AF540713

Higher Education in The 21st Century

Vision and Action

HIGHER EDUCATION IN THE 21st CENTURY

(Vision and Action)

Editor

Dr. Digumarti Bhaskara Rao

M.Sc., M.A., M.A., M.Ed., Ph.D.
R.V.R. College of Education
D–43, S.V.N. Colony
Guntur—2522006
Andhra Pradesh

DISCOVERY PUBLISHING HOUSE
NEW DELHI

Published by:

DISCOVERY PUBLISHING HOUSE PVT. LTD.
4383/4B, Ansari Road, Darya Ganj
New Delhi-110 002 (India)
Phone : +91-11-23279245; 23253475; 43596065
E-mail : discoverybooksindia@gmail.com
discoverypublishinghouse@gmail.com
namitwasan9@gmail.com
web : www.discoverypublishinggroup.com

First Published: 2003

Reprinted: 2022

ISBN: 978-81-7141-688-2

Higher Education in the 21st Century:
Vision and Action

Printed at:
Infinity Imaging Systems
Delhi

To
a great statesman

Dr. Kasaraneni Sadasiva Rao
(M.S.)

Former Member of Legislative Assembly
Andhra Pradesh

Foreword

For the world of education, science and culture, the dates from 5 to 9 October 1998 will go down in history as the period of the first-ever World Conference on Higher Education. Representatives of 182 States responsible for education and higher education, teachers, researchers, students members of parliament, representatives of intergovernmental and non-governmental organisations from various sectors of society, the world of work and business, financial organisations, publishing houses, etc.—in all more than 4,000 participants—have come to Paris to discuss matters of higher education and to agree on the higher education we need for the next century: f· : whom, with whom, and why, for what kind of society and what kind of world.

No conference convened until now by UNESCO has brought together such a large number of participants non—I believe I can safely say—has represented society as fully as this World Conference on Higher Education. These past five days have seen the largest international gathering on higher education held this century.

The interest shown by such widely different circles from across the world in the work of the Conference is the expression of a clear realisation of the growing importance of education, and in particular of higher education, for the destiny of humankind and society itself. In a world in which inequalities between nations and countries are growing more acute, where economic considerations dominate and the absolute power of money and the pursuit of profit at all costs brush aside ethical values and all sense of human solidarity, and where violence, far from retreating, proliferates in various and often hitherto unknown forms, and thus constitutes a real threat of civil and international peace, all education systems, and higher education in particular, are directly challenged.

It is no longer necessary to demonstrate the importance of education and higher education for sustainable, endogenous development, for democracy and peace, for a strengthening of the defence of peace as a human value, and for the respect and protection of all human rights and fundamental freedoms. The far-reaching changes now taking place in the world, and the entry of human values into a society based on knowledge and information, reveal how overwhelmingly important education and higher education are. It is appropriate to note, as the head of the one of the delegations to the Conference has said, that "science and education are what will determine the future will-being of individuals and of nations." And it is above all within the framework of higher education that science and education meet, unite and stimulate one another, by advancing and disseminating knowledge. Because one of the tasks of higher education is to educate the educators, to further research into education and to make recommendations about the content, methods and organisation of education at each of its different levels and in its various forms, higher education has a decisive contribution to make to the progress of the educational task within society towards lifelong education for all.

When I opened this Conference, I expressed the wish that we might make the completion of the long process of preparation for it a new beginning, that we might gather its harvest in order the better to use it, like food and seed, and that our Conference might plant the seeds of better education for the twenty-first century.

And that is what the Conference has done. It has answered the questions that were asked of it. It has set the direction needed to prepare higher education for the tasks that await it in the twenty-first century, and to help humankind, society and the community of nations to stride out towards a better future, towards a world more just, more humane, more caring and more peaceful. The Conference has established the principles and determined the ways to achieving this in the texts of the World Declaration and the Framework for Priority Action adopted at the close to its deliberations.

Several factors have come together to enable the Conference, despite different national and regional situations, to adopt texts of particular importance, which concern all participants. It is the result of the work of five regional conferences, which took place in Havana, Dakar, Tokyo, Palermo and Beirut between 1996 and 1998. It is the result of the reflections and the commitment of vice-chancellors and presidents, and of the teachers, staff and students of universities and other institutions of higher education. It is also, and above all, the result of active and constructive enrolment by a number of States in various regions and by many intergovernmental and non-governmental organisations in the process of the development of draft declarations and action plans in particular within the framework of the two stages of consultation which preceded the Conference. It is largely the result of participants' commitment to opening up ways of renewing and transforming higher education in the direction that the history and development of the world require. It is the result of the will and the remarkable spirit of cooperation that everyone has shown throughout this Conference. Lastly, it is the result of the objective fact that, in the field of higher education, there is greater convergence and a greater community of problems, trends, challenges and concerns than national and regional differences and specificities would suggest, although the problems confronting many developing countries are more serious and more urgent than those experienced by the industrialised countries.

In their scope, in their global vision of the problems of higher education and in their constructive approach, the texts adopted by this first World Conference are probably without precedent.

This Conference has provided a forum for a wealth of debates and exchanges of views, and I should like to raise here some of the main ideas which have emerged from them.

The Conference was unanimous in considering that a **renewal** of higher education is essential for the whole of society to be able to face up to the challenges of the twenty-first century, to ensure its intellectual independence, to create and advance knowledge, and to educate and train responsible, enlightened citizens and qualified specialists, without whom no nation can progress economically, socially, culturally or politically.

As the Declaration of the World Conference emphasizes, since society is "increasingly **knowledge-based** (...), higher education and research now act as essential components of cultural, socio-economic and environmentally sustainable development of individuals, communities and nations." The development of higher education must therefore feature among the highest national priorities.

It is now clear that, to fulfil its mission, **higher education must change** radically, by becoming organically flexible, and at the same time more diverse in its institutions, its structures, its curricula, and the nature and forms of its programmes and delivery systems, and by mastering the information technologies which can help it achieve its purpose. Higher education must anticipate the developing needs of society and individuals, and it must be open to the needs of adults for continuing education and the updating of their knowledge and skills, whether in the pursuit of retraining, redeployment or cultural improvement in general. In short, **higher education in the twenty-first century must be seen to be part of the global project of continuing education for all,** it must become the motivating force of that project, the place where it all happens, and it must help to integrate into that project all other levels and forms of education by strengthening its links with them.

One central question which was present throughout the debates, and which is closely related to the preceding one, is that of **access** to higher education. This principle has been clearly defined by the World Declaration, which was itself inspired by the great prescriptive texts of the United Nations and above all by Article 26 of the Universal Declaration of Human Rights.[1] "Admission to higher education," the Declaration of the World Conference stipulates, "should be founded on the merit, capacity, efforts, perseverance and devotion showed by those seeking access to it, and can take place in a lifelong scheme, at any time, with due recognition of previously acquired skills". **The concern for equity** in this respect, strongly emphasised in the Universal Declaration of Human Rights, the UNESCO Convention against Discrimination in Education (1960) and the International Covenant on Economic, Social and Cultural Rights (1966), as **the first principle** governing access to higher education, is vigorously reaffirmed by the World Conference in its Declaration. It is the duty of al States, and of all those who have taken part in the Conference, to work, with the support of UNESCO, to promote the relevant provisions of the Declaration through legislative and national regulatory channels and through actual educational practice.

All citizens must be aware that, as stated in the Universal Declaration of Human Rights, it is the merit and effort of the individual which should determine access to higher education. Anyone who possesses the "merit" and the means may be admitted to higher education, and is expected to contribute financially to the institution providing it; anyone who possess the "merit" but not the means may be admitted to higher education, but society provides for its financing; lastly, anyone who possesses the means but not the "merit" must endeavour to acquire the "merit" and to have it recognised in order to enter higher education, which thus becomes a permanent

---

1. "Everyone has the right to education. Education shall be free, at least in the elementary and fundamental stages. Elementary education shall be compulsory. Technical and professional education shall be made generally available **and higher education shall be equally accessible to all on the basis of merit."** [Article 26 (1)].

space for higher learning. From élite-based to merit-based: these words accurately express, in my opinion, the new face of higher education.

Beyond these general principles governing access, the debates revealed particular emphasis on certain points. Above all, the importance of continuing and intensifying our efforts to extend and improve access for women to all areas of higher education, especially to scientific and technological studies, to teaching positions in higher education and to management responsibilities.

Another point concerning equity and social justice emerges from the discussions of the Conference. Economic, social and educational measures and needed throughout the educational careers of children and young people from underprivileged backgrounds and modest circumstances to enable them to acquire the necessary preparations for access to and success in higher education.

Lastly, Conference participants were clearly inspired by this same concern when they recommended appropriate measures to eliminate discrimination and to overcome the inequalities concerning access to higher education suffered by the disabled, minorities, refugees and peoples displaced following natural disasters or conflicts.

The question of access takes on a new dimension as we approach the twenty-first century which will necessarily transform higher education and see the implementation of lifelong learning **for all.** The popularisation of higher education, frequently mentioned during the debates, is only one manifestation of a marked trend, already well-established in the industrialised countries, and which appears to be irreversible in the long term. It is interesting to note in this respect that gross enrolment ratios in higher education in developed regions had already reached almost 60 per cent by 1995, and in North America 84 per cent. Overall, in developing countries, enrolment ratios rose between 1960 and 1995 from 1.8 per cent to 8.9 per cent and teacher numbers in the same period increased by a factor of more than eleven, revealing growth rates much higher than those observed in the developed countries. It should be added in this respect that these figures take only partially into account those adults taking various non-traditional post-secondary courses offered by establishments of higher education and other public or private organisations.

Several factors combine to produce this spectacular development in higher education. The expansion of secondary education is one of the most prominent. Although it has not reached the growth rates of higher education, secondary education is growing at a pace no less significant. Between 1960 and 1995, its students numbers worldwide increased from 91 million to 372 million, and gross enrolment ratios at secondary level doubled, from 29 per cent to 58 per cent. In the developed countries, where enrolment ratios have reached 99 per cent, secondary education has become almost universal. In developing countries during the same period, student numbers were multiplied by 6.7 and gross enrolment ratios have almost tripled. Everywhere, numbers of young graduates of secondary education have increased relentlessly. However, in very many countries, most students in the secondary sector are concentrated in general subjects areas where curriculum content to often continues to be designed solely to prepare students for entry into higher education. This leads many young people, on completion of their secondary studies, to move into higher education simply because they have not been prepared to enter the world of work. Not possessing any other skills, those graduates of secondary education who, for one reason or another, do not enter higher education are confronted with the risk of unemployment.

This situation, the far-reaching changes which higher education needs to undergo and the prospect of lifelong learning for all (which implies the possibility of lifelong access to higher education at any age, to supplement or bring up to date students' general or specialised skills, and/or to retrain or acquire new skills), create the need to reconsider the overall design of secondary education. The secondary sector must have **a twofold objective:** to prepare for the world of work and at the same time to prepare for the entry into higher education. This twofold objective will enable us to define the spirit and content of secondary education for the twenty-first century, its diversification and the role at this level to education of technical and vocational training.

The combined effect of the expansion of secondary education, the steady increase in the number and the proportion of jobs and professional activities which require high-level knowledge and skills, and the continuing increase in the need for higher studies and advanced learning, for updating knowledge, retraining and redeployment, is that, in the more or less long term according to country, practically everyone will undergo, at some time or other in life and probably more than once, post-secondary higher education in one form or another. In this sense, it is possible to speak to a trend towards the generalisation of higher education, which will be supported and facilitated by a better mastery of information and communication technologies and increasingly broad use of these. This generalisation will not result in a direct transition for all from secondary to higher education. It will be achieved using increasingly diversified methods, at different times in life, through curricula with different purposes, access routes and durations, an which will be increasingly varied, with studies within and institutionalised framework alternating with self teaching and other forms of learning.

It is with this future in view that access to higher education will be widened, popularised and made more equitable, and efforts will be made to promote equal opportunities for success in higher studies.

The necessary transition of higher education into a space for higher learning in which everyone will be able to enjoy more flexible access at any age for intensive training, updating knowledge and the acquisition of new skills, or for the purposes of redeployment, constitutes one of the main aspects of the democratisation and the renovation of higher education and education in general. At the same time, this development will make higher education an ideal meeting-place for the sharing of knowledge and the mutual enrichment of teachers at all levels.

Two other key ideas appear to me to deserve mention at this point: that of **the mission** of higher education, and that of how it should be opened up to the whole of society as a means of promoting **interaction** between the principal social actors and the main sectors of the economy.

As regards the mission of higher education, the debates have shown that it needs to be widened. Beyond its **traditional functions of teaching, training, research and study, all of which remain fundamental,** many heads of delegation made a point of asserting the importance of the educational mission of higher education, which consists in **promoting development of the whole person and training responsible, informed citizens, committed to working for a better society in the future.** Higher education also has **a contribution to make to the solution of the major problems of planetary, regional and local importance** (poverty, homelessness, worsening inequalities, environmental degradation, etc.), and to work to promote development, the sharing of knowledge, solidarity, the universal respect of human rights, democracy, equality of rights between women and men and a culture of peace and non-violence. The Conference stressed very strongly **the cultural and ethical mission** of higher education, which, in the age in which we live, is one of the highest priorities of education in general.

On the vast subject of **the interaction of higher education with society,** I will confine myself here to mentioning, briefly, three points. The first relates to the relationship between higher education and the State, and society as a whole. The Conference has reaffirmed, as the essential condition enabling higher education to fulfil its mission, that institutional **autonomy** and **academic freedoms** must be guaranteed and respected by the State and society. The **corollary** is the duty placed on institutions of higher education **to account** to society for their activities and the use of the resources placed at their disposal. In this context also, the responsibility of the State for the financing of higher education as an essential public service, as well as the need for society to support it, were strongly reaffirmed by a number of speakers. At the same time, they emphasised the importance for institutions of higher education of securing additional sources of financing, implementing revenue-generating activities, strengthening their management, adopting forward-looking management practices to that end and using their resources in a more rational and more effective way. These positions are clearly emphasised in the Declaration of the Conference. The question of **financing** will clearly be **one of the major challenges** of the years to come.

This problem is particularly acutely felt in many developing countries, and measures aimed solely at reinforcing management and using resources more rationally will not be sufficient to solve it. A revision of national budget priorities also deserves to be envisaged. Other measures are necessary in order to make it possible for developing countries to release additional resources for education and for the solution of many social problems.[2]

Another major point which was widely commented upon relates to the interaction between higher education and **the world of work.** It is important that this interaction be

2. The resources of many developing countries are to a large extent mortgaged by the burden of debt servicing and repayment. In 27 countries, debt exceeds GDP. Between 1990 and 1995, the countries of sub-Saharan Africa devoted on average 12 billion dollars per annum to debt repayment, whereas their total levels of indebtedness increased by 33 billion dollars. Some of these countries devote to debt repayment amounts practically equivalent to the totality of the government aid they receive for their development. In adopting at its twenty-fifth session the International Development Strategy for the Second Development Decade, the General Assembly of the United Nations fixed the objective for official development assistance by the industrialised countries at 0.70 per cent of their GNP. This objective of solidarity, since then confirmed several times is far from having been achieved. In an interdependent world, solidarity is not only an ethical requirement. It is also a political necessity.

conceived as **a partnership, a relationship of equals,** not as the subordination of one of the other. I would like to quote here Mr Lionel Jospin, Prime Minister of France, who challenged "the mercantile attitude whereby [higher education] could be market-led. (...) In this field, as in others," he declared, "the market economy is a fact of life within which we act. But it should not form the horizon of society. The market is an instrument is not the *raison-d'-étre* of democracy."

* * *

One of the speakers said in his contribution that **student enrolment in the business of higher education** is healthy, even though it may sometimes be "noisy". The Conference heard an **important declaration** from the representative of student organisations. That declaration expressed students' awareness of their responsibility for their studies, but also their responsibility for society and in society. This is good to hear, and we should make the point strongly that their participation, and that of their organisations, in everything that relates to higher education, are essential.

* * *

In adopting its Declaration and the Framework for Priority Action, the World Conference has laid the foundations that will **guide the development of national higher education policies** for the next country. The Conference has also promoted the emergence of an alliance between the university and educational communities and their principal partners within society. Parliaments, as the voice of the people, have an important role to play in consolidating this alliance and in making it widely known and affective. The time has now come for action, and I am pleased to note, as I meet with heads of state and government, ministers of education and higher education, and Permanent Delegates to UNESCO, that in their efforts to design and implement higher education reforms, Member States are beginning to draw inspiration from the orientations contained in the texts adopted by the World Conference.

Much will now depend on the speed of reaction of all those in the alliance—individuals and institutions—who must work together to promote change in higher education. UNESCO took the initiative of lunching the process which led to the World Conference. UNESCO will do its best **to ensure** in close cooperation with higher education authorities and the IGOs and NGOs concerned, **that the actions now to be undertaken are pursued as effectively as possible.** For my part, I have already taken a series of measures within the Organisation to ensure that follow-up action to the World Conference will be given all necessary impetus.

We stand at the beginning of a new century and a new millennium. It is symbolic that they should have been preceded by the **International Year for the Culture of Peace,** which will be immediately followed by the International Decade for a Culture of Peace and Non-Violence for the Children of the World (2001-2010), both proclaimed by the General Assembly of the United Nations. In the Declaration adopted by the World Conference, the point is made that "on the threshold of a new millennium to is the duty of higher education to ensure that the values and the ideals of a culture of peace prevail". It is of the greatest importance that, true to their humanistic traditions and to their vocations, institutions of higher education the world over, their teachers, students and organisations, should be among the most active and the most committed of all those who will mark the Year and the International Decade by their efforts to promote a culture of peace and non-violence. May this Year and this Decade serve in particular to implement long-term programmes of action for solidarity, one of the fundamental values of a culture of peace, to the benefit of the institutions, teachers and students of the developing countries

Federico Mayor

Preface

With an objective of laying down the fundamental principles for the in-depth reform of higher education systems throughout the world, and with an intention to contribute to transforming higher education, in its material and virtual manifestations, into an environment for lifelong learning, for cultural debate, and for the affirmation and safeguarding of diversity for the intellectual and moral solidarity of mankind, the UNESCO convened the World Conference on Higher Education at UNESCO headquarters in Paris from 5 to 9 October 1998.

The World Conference on Higher Education first ever conference for the world of education which brought together the representatives of 182, countries responsible for education and higher education teachers, researchers, students, members of parliament, representatives of inter-governmental and non-governmental organisations from various sectors of society, the world of work and business, financial organisations, publishing houses, etc. They discussed the matters of higher education and agreed on the higher education we need for the twenty-first century: for whom with whom, and why, for what kind of society and what kind of world.

The Conference set the direction needed to prepare higher education for the tasks to help human kind, society and the community of nations to stride out towards a better future, towards a world more just, more humane, more caring and more peaceful.

The declarations adopted at the World Conference on Higher Education and at the regional conferences, and the summaries of the commissions and debates will guide in realising the core missions of higher education-to educate, to train, to undertake research, and to provide services to the community-throughout the world.

Bhaskara Rao

Acknowledgements

I
express my sincere thanks to
the UNESCO, Paris, France

Mr. Federico Mayor, Former D-G of UNESCO

Komlavi F. Seddoh, UNESCO

Ana Font Giner, UNESCO

Division of Higher Education, UNESCO

Unit for the WCHE Follow-up UNESCO

Department for Education and Employment, UK

UNESCO-BREDA, Dakar, Senegal

UNESCO-UNEBDAS, Beirut, Lebanon

UNESCO-PROAP, Bangkok, Thailand

UNESCO-CEPES, Bucharest, Romania

UNESCO-CRESALC, Caracas, Venezula

For utilising their documents
in preparing this book
for the benefit of
higher education enterprise.

EDITOR

Dr. Digumarti Bhaskara Rao

Contents

Part IV
Thematic Debates

Part I

World Conference on Higher Education

1

World Conference on Higher Education

In convening the World Conference on Higher Education (Paris, 5-9 October 1998), UNESCO's objective was to lay down the fundamental principles for the in-depth reform of higher education systems throughout the world. In our complex and rapidly changing global society, higher education must contribute to the building of peace founded on a process of development and predicated on equity, justice, solidarity and liberty. To attain this objective, access on the basis of merit, the renovation of systems and institutions, and service to society, including closer links to the world of work, must be the basis of renewal and renovation in this level of education. This requires that higher education enjoy autonomy and freedom exercised with responsibility.

When calling the Conference, Federico Mayor, the Director-General UNESCO, had in mind that this initiative should contribute to transforming higher education, in its material and virtual manifestations, into an environmental for lifelong learning, for cultural debate, for the affirmation and safeguarding of diversity, and for forging and confirming the values and principles laid down in the constitution of UNESCO for "the intellectual and moral solidarity of mankind".

The analysis made by ministers and heads of delegations during the conference, the positive comments of the Executive

Board of UNESCO immediately after the World Conference and the actions being taken all over the world by governments to include the principles of the Declaration in their policy statements and decisions concerning higher education show that the Conference gave the international community a powerful instrument to facilitate the reform of higher education.

The basis for these initiatives lies in the principle that higher education shall be equally accessible to all on the basis of merit, in keeping with Article 26.1 of the Universal Declaration on Human Rights. As accepted by all participants at the conference, no discrimination can be accepted in granting access to higher education on grounds of race, gender, language, religion or economic, cultural or social distinctions or physical disabilities.

The core missions of higher education—to educate, to train, to undertake research and to provide services to the community—must be preserved, reinforced and further expanded. The World Conference stressed that higher education institutions must seek to educate qualified graduates who are responsible citizens and to provide opportunities for higher learning throughout life At the end of this century, we can car"' see the devastating effects of a concept of economic development based on speculation. Thus, the adoption by the international community of a document stating clearly that higher education institutions must preserve their critical functions in the interest of democracy is timely and this must be taken seriously by policy-makers.

Relevance cannot be an abstract concept. As the Conference declared, relevance "should be assessed in terms of the fit between what society expects of institutions and what they do". In particular, relationships with the world of work should be based on long-term orientations and societal aims and needs, as well as on respect for cultures and environmental protection. Relevance means also a better integration of higher education into the whole education system: The Conference insisted on "the reordering of its links with all levels of education, in particular with secondary education" as a priority.

The search for quality is indispensable for a policy based on merit. But quality must be linked in a given context to relevance and to the solution of problems of the community, and assessments of quality should embrace all functions and activities of higher education. In this the role of research is especially essential. This will be the main subject of the World Conference on Science that UNESCO is organising (July 1999, Budapest), Research must be enhanced in all disciplines as an instrument for the advancement of knowledge through approaches reinforcing interdisciplinarity, transdisciplinarity and innovation. In the follow-up of both world conferences, we would like to see the expansion and networking of Centres and Chairs on Higher Education and on Science Policy in each region.

The Conference statements regarding the role of staff, in particular teachers, the importance of the involvement of students in the decision process and the measures that should be taken or reinforced to ensure the participation of women in higher education, constitute essential points of these documents and must serve as a guide to policy-makers and to all who have responsibilities in their implementation

Finally, a key philosophical point but with concrete impact is the statement made by the Conference that higher education should be considered as a public good. Equally important is the affirmation that the international dimension of higher education is an inherent part of its quality. UNESCO gave the example with the launching of the UNITWIN/UNESCO Chairs Programme and its work on the recognition of studies, degrees and diplomas, based on close partnership, solidarity and co-operation among equals.

As stated in the preamble of the Declaration, the second half of this century will go down in the history of higher education as the period of its most spectacular expansion. The analysis of the implications of this reality was made by the **UNESCO Policy Paper for Change and Development in**

Higher Education launched in 1995. This document showed also that as we come to the end of the twentieth century, there are still flagrant inequalities in higher education, and a growing gap between the industrialised countries and the so-called developing countries.

In convening the World Conference on Higher Education, UNESCO reaffirmed its strong 50-year-old commitment to fostering the development of higher education and research. The Conference sought to generate a broad debate on higher education to complement other major conferences in the field of education that constitute landmarks in the process of its renewal notably the World Conference on Education for All (Jomtien, Thailand, 1990), the 45th session of the International Conference on Education on the Role of Teachers in a Changing World (Geneva, 1996) and the International Conference on Adult Education (Hamburg, 1997). In addition, the World Conference reiterated the recommendations relating to the opening up of higher education of the International Commission on Education for the Twenty-first Century, **Learning: The Treasure Within** (1996).

The Conference was preceded by a widespread mobilisation of partners, of national policy-makers, institutional leaders, the professorate and researchers, including those involved in the UNITWIN/UNESCO Chairs Programme, the student community, and the economic and professional sectors as well as the civil society, including parliamentarians.

Regional Conferences were held in Havana in November 1996 (Latin America and the Caribbean), Dakar in April 1997 (Africa), Tokyo in July 1997 (Asia and the Pacific), Palermo in September 1997 (Europe) and Beirut in March 1998 (Arab States). The results of these conferences, their declarations and their plans of action were taken into consideration in the preparation of the documents adopted at the World Conference and were included in this report. The findings of these conferences were also utilised for the working documents and constituted the main base for the discussions of the Commissions of the Conference on **relevance, quality,**

management and financing, and international co-operation. They confirmed that we are now facing global problems that call for solutions to be applied worldwide, even though in every region there are variations in the economic, social, cultural and political context. UNESCO will publish a series of documents, including one on the work of the Commissions.

The results of the regional conferences were complemented by studies and analyses undertaken by some fifty governmental and non-governmental organisations charged with preparing a series of thematic debates on important issues on higher education at the end of this century. Twelve debates were structured in relation with three main domains:

Higher education and development

- The requirements of the world of work,
- Higher education and sustainable human development,
- Contributing to national and regional development,
- Higher education staff development: a continuing mission.

New trends and innovations in higher education

- Higher education for a new society: a student vision,
- From traditional to virtual: the new information technologies,
- Higher education and research: challenges and opportunities,
- The contribution of higher education to the education system as a whole.

Higher education, culture and society

- Women and higher education: issues and perspectives,
- Promoting a culture of peace,

- Mobilising the power of culture,
- Autonomy, social responsibility and academic freedom.

The Thematic Debates raised a great interest among Conference participants. Their results will be disseminated separately.

In addition to the commissions and thematic debates, a series of special lectures and at plenary sessions speeches from ministers and chiefs of delegation reported on what is happening in their countries in the field of higher education and expressed their position on the themes of the conference. The Ministers addressed the following issues:

- The changing missions of higher education in the twenty-first century,
- Interaction of higher education with society,
- The impact of the change process on higher education, diversification and increased flexibility of systems, and their promotion of lifelong learning,
- Access to higher education.

All these contributions were taken into consideration in the final version of the Declaration and Framework for Action as well as the comments of all Member States, inter-governmental and non-governmental organisations with an interest in higher education, or invited to attend the Conference.

There is no doubt that the documents the participants adopted at the end of the conference, the "World Declaration on Higher Education for the Twenty-first Century: Vision and Action" and the "Framework for Priority Action for Change and Development of Higher Education" represent an agreement between all stakeholders concerning the principal and key actions needed for the renewal of higher education in the twenty-first century. Now comes the time for action, for the execution of projects, for developing international co-operation based on solidarity and the building of an equitable society, in particular through research, training of specialists and community projects aiming at eliminating poverty, violence, illiteracy, hunger, intolerance, environmental degradation and disease, and the development of a culture of peace.

The World Declaration and the Framework for Priority Action will help set up the agenda both for higher education policy-making in Member States and for development strategies to be established or further strengthened by UNESCO and its partners.

As a result of the Conference process, a new coalition between the higher education community and its major partners has emerged. Contacts with Chiefs of states, Ministers of Education and Higher Education and delegates of UNESCO showed clearly the they have already started to utilize these documents in the implementation of reforms in higher education.

The long-term outcome of the Conference will be the efficient and effective renovation and renewal of higher education systems and institutions based on the principles of relevance and quality, and with a commitment to enhanced international co-operation and academic solidarity.

Much now depends on the dynamism of the coalition of all those—individuals and institutions—involved in the process of change in higher education. UNESCO took the responsibility of launching the process which culminated with the World Conference. UNESCO will make its best efforts to ensure an efficient follow-up, jointly with higher education authorities, intergovernmental organisations and non-governmental organisations interested in higher education.

2

World Declaration on Higher Education for the Twenty-first Century:

Vision and Action

PREAMBLE

On the eve of a new century, there is an **unprecedented demand for and a great diversification in higher education, as well as an increased awareness of its vital importance for sociocultural and economic development,** and for building the future, for which the younger generations will need to be equipped with new skills, knowledge and ideals. Higher education includes 'all types of studies, training or training for research at the post-secondary level, provided by universities or other educational establishments that are approved as institutions of higher education by the competent State authorities'.[1] Everywhere higher education is faced with great challenges and difficulties related to financing, equity of conditions at access into and during the course of studies, improved staff development, skills-based training, enhancement and preservation of equality in teaching, research and services, relevance of programmes, employability of graduates, establishment of

1. Definition approved by the General Conference of UNESCO at its 27th session (November 1993) in the Recommendation on the Recognition of Studies and Qualifications in Higher Education.

efficient co-operation agreements and equitable access to the benefits of international co-operation. At the same time, higher education is being challenged by new opportunities relating to technologies that are improving the ways in which knowledge can be produced, managed, disseminated, accessed and controlled. Equitable access to these technologies should be ensured at all levels of education systems.

The second half of this century will go down in the history of higher education as the period of its most spectacular **expansion:** an over sixfold increase in student enrolments worldwide, from 13 million in 1960 to 82 million in 1995. But it is also the period which has seen the gap between industrially developed, **the developing countries and in particular the least developed countries** with regard to access and resources for higher learning and research, already enormous, becoming even wider. It has also been a period of increased socio-economic stratification and greater difference in educational opportunity within countries, including in some of the most developed and wealthiest nations. Without adequate higher education and research institutions providing a critical mass of skilled and educated people, no country can ensure genuine endogenous and sustainable development and, in particular, developing countries and least developed countries cannot reduce the gap separating them from the industrially developed ones. Sharing knowledge, international co-operation and new technologies can offer new opportunities to reduce this gap.

Higher education has given ample proof of its viability over the centuries and of its ability to change and to induce chance and progress in society. Owing to the scope and pace of change, society has become increasingly **knowledge-based** so that higher learning and research now act as essential components to cultural, socio-economic and environmentally sustainable development of individuals, communities and nations. Higher education itself is confronted therefore with formidable challenges and must proceed to the most radical **change and renewal it has ever been required** to undertake, so that our society, which is currently undergoing a profound crisis of values, can transcend mere economic considerations and incorporate deeper dimensions of morality and spirituality.

It is with the aim of providing solutions to these challenges and of setting in motion a process of in-depth reform in higher education worldwide that UNESCO has convened a World Conference on Higher Education in the Twenty-First Century: Vision and Action. In preparation for the Conference, UNESCO issued, in 1995, its *Policy Paper for Change and Development in Higher Education.* Five regional consultations (Havana, November 1996; Dakar, April 1997; Tokyo, July 1997; Palermo, September 1997; and Beirut, March 1998) were subsequently held. The Declarations and Plans of Action adopted by them, each preserving its own specificity, are duly taken into account in the present Declaration—as is the whole process of reflection undertaken by the preparation of the World Conference—and are annexed to it.

***

We, participants in the World Conference on Higher Education, assembled at UNESCO Headquarters in Paris, from 5 to 9 October 1998,

Recalling the principles of the Charter of the United Nations, the Universal Declaration of Human Rights, the International Covenant on Economic, Social and Cultural Rights, and the International Covenant on Civil and Political Rights,

Recalling also the Universal Declaration of Human Rights which states in Article 26, paragraph 1, that 'Everyone has the right to education' and that 'higher education shall be equally accessible to all on the basis of merit', and *endorsing* the basic principles of the Convention against Discrimination in Education (1960), which, by Article 4, commits the States Parties to it to 'make higher education equally accessible to all on the basis of individual capacity',

Taking into account the recommendations concerning higher education of major commissions and conferences, *inter alia,* the International Commission on Education for the

Twenty-First Century, the World Commission on Culture and Development, the 44th and 45th sessions of the International Conference on Education (Geneva, 1994 and 1996), the decisions taken at the 27th and 29th sessions of UNESCO's General Conference, in particular regarding the Recommendation concerning the Status of Higher-Education Teaching Personnel, the World Conference on Education for All (Jomtien, Thailand, 1990), the United Nations Conference on Environment and Development (Rio de Janeiro, 1992), the Conference on Academic Freedom and University Autonomy (Sinaia, 1992), the World Conference on Human Rights (Vienna, 1993) the World Summit for Social Development (Copenhagen, 1995), the fourth World Conference on Women (Beijing, 1995), the International Congress on Education and Informatics (Moscow, 1996), the World Congress on Higher Education and Human Resources Development for the Twenty-First Century (Manila, 1997), the fifth International Conference on Adult Education (Hamburg, 1997) and especially the Agenda for the Future under Theme 2 (Improving the conditions and quality of learning) starting: 'We commit ourselves to ... opening schools, colleges and universities to adult learners ... by calling upon the World Conference on Higher Education (Paris, 1998) to promote the transformation of post-secondary institutions into lifelong learning institutions and to define the role of universities accordingly',

Convinced that education is a fundamental pillar of human rights, democracy, sustainable development and peace, and shall therefore become accessible to all throughout life and that measures are required to ensure co-ordination and co-operation across and between the various sectors, particularly between general, technical and professional secondary and post-secondary education as well as between universities, colleges and technical institutions,

Believing that, in this context, the solution of the problems faced on the eve of the twenty-first century will be determined by the vision of the future society and by the role that is assigned to education in general and to higher education in particular,

Aware that on the threshold of a new millennium it is the duty of higher education to ensure that the values and ideals of a culture of peace prevail and that the intellectual community should be mobilised to the end,

Considering that a substantial change and development of higher, education, the enhancement of its quality and relevance, and the solution to the major challenges it faces, require the strong involvement not only of governments and of higher education institutions, but also of all stakeholders, including students and their families, teachers, business and industry, the public and private sectors of the economy, parliaments, the media, the community, professional associations and society as well as a greater responsibility of higher education institutions towards society and accountability in the use of public and private, national or international resources,

Emphasising that higher education systems should enhance their capacity to live with uncertainty, to change and bring about change, and to address social needs and to promote solidarity and equity; should preserve and exercise scientific rigour and originality, in a spirit of impartiality, as a basic prerequisite for attaining and sustaining an indispensable level of quality; and should place students at the centre of their concerns, **within a lifelong perspective,** so as to allow their full integration into the global knowledge society of the coming century,

Also believing that international co-operation and exchange are major avenues for advancing higher education throughout the world.

Proclaim the following:

MISSIONS AND FUNCTIONS OF HIGHER EDUCATION

Article 1. Mission to educate, to train and to undertake research

We affirm that the core missions and values of higher education, in particular the mission to contribute to the sustainable development and improvement of society as a whole, should be preserved, reinforced and further expanded, namely, to:

(a) educate highly qualified graduates and responsible citizens able to meet the needs of all sectors of human activity, by offering relevant qualifications, including professional training, which combine high-level knowledge and skills, using courses and content continually tailored to the present and future needs of society;

(b) provide opportunities (*espace ouvert*) **for higher learning and for learning throughout life,** giving to learners and optimal range of choice and a flexibility of entry and exit poir⁺s within the system, as well as an opportunity for individual development and social mobility in **order to educate for citizenship and for active participation in society,** with a worldwide vision, for endogenous capacity-building, and for the consolidation of human rights, sustainable development, democracy and peace, in a context of justice;

(c) **advance, create and disseminate knowledge through research** and provide, as part of its service to he community, relevant expertise to assist societies in cultural, social and economic development, promoting and developing scientific and technological research as well as research in the social sciences, the humanities and the creative arts;

(d) help **understand, interpret, preserve, enhance, promote and disseminate national and regional, international and historic cultures,** in a context of cultural pluralism and diversity;

(e) help protect and enhance **societal values** by training young people in the values which form the basis of democratic citizenship and by providing critical and detached perspectives to assist in the discussion of strategic options and th reinforcement of humanistic perspective;

(f) contribute to the development and improvement of education at all levels, including through the training of teachers.

Article 2. Ethical role, autonomy, responsibility and anticipatory function

In accordance with the Recommendation concerning the Status of Higher-Education Teaching Personnel approved by the General Conference of UNESCO in November 1997, **higher education institutions and their personnel and students should:**

(a) preserve and develop their crucial functions, through the exercise of ethics and scientific and intellectual rigour in their various activities;

(b) be able to speak out on ethical, cultural and social problems completely independently and in full awareness of their responsibilities, exercising a kind of intellectual authority that society needs to help it to reflect, understand and act;

(c) enhance their critical and forward-looking functions, through continuing analysis of emerging social, economic, cultural and political trends, providing a focus for forecasting, warning and prevention;

(d) exercise their intellectual capacity and their moral prestige to defend and actively disseminate universally accepted values, including peace, justice, freedom, equality and solidarity, as enshrined in UNESCO'. Constitution;

(e) enjoy full academic autonomy and freedom, conceived as a set of rights and duties, while being fully responsible and accountable to society;

(f) play a role in helping identify and address issues that affect the well-being of communities, nations and global society.

SHAPING A NEW VISION OF HIGHER EDUCATION

Article 3. Equity of access

(a) In keeping with Article 26.1 of the Universal Declaration of Human Rights, admission to higher

education should be based on the merit, capacity, efforts, perseverance and devotion, showed by those seeking access to it, and can take place in a lifelong scheme, at any time, with due recognition of previously acquired skills. As a consequence, no discrimination can be accepted in granting access to higher education on grounds of race, gender, language or religion, or economic, cultural or social distinctions, or physical disabilities.

(b) Equity of access to higher education should begin with the reinforcement and, if need be, the reordering of its likes with all other levels of education, particularly with secondary education. Higher education institutions must be viewed as, and must work within themselves to be a part of and encourage, a seamless system starting with early childhood and primary education and continuing through life. Higher education institutions must work in active partnership with parents, schools, students, socio-economic groups and communities. Secondary education should not only prepare qualified candidates for access to higher education by developing the capacity to learn on a board basis but also open the way to active life by providing training on a wide range of jobs. However, access to higher education should remain open to those successfully completing secondary school, or its equivalent, or presenting entry qualifications, as far as possible, at any age and without any discrimination.

(c) As a consequence, the rapid and wide-reaching demand for higher education requires, where appropriate, **all policies concerning access to higher education** to give priority in the future to the approach based on the merit of the individual, as defined in Article 3(a) above.

(d) Access to higher education for members of some special target groups, such as indigenous peoples, cultural and linguistic minorities, disadvantaged

groups, peoples living under occupation and those who suffer from disabilities, must be actively facilitated, since these groups as collectivities and as individuals may have both experience and talent that can be of great value for the development of societies and nations. Special material help and educational solutions can help overcome the obstacles that these groups face, both in accessing and in continuing higher education.

Article 4. Enhancing participation and promoting the role of women

(a) Although significant progress has been achieved to enhance the **access of women** to higher education, various socio-economic, cultural and political obstacles continue in many places in the world to impede their full access and effective integration. To overcome them remains and urgent priority in the renewal process for ensuring an equitable and non-discriminatory system of higher education based on the principle of merit.

(b) Further efforts are required to eliminate all gender stereotyping in higher education, to consider gender aspects in different disciplines and to consolidate women's participation at all levels and in all disciplines, in which they are under-represented and, in particular, to enhance their active involvement in decision-making.

(c) Gender studies (women's studies) should be promoted as a field of knowledge, strategic for the transformation of higher education and society.

(d) Efforts should be made to eliminate political and social barriers whereby women are under-represented and in particular to enhance their active involvement at policy and decision-making levels within higher education and society.

Article 5. Advancing knowledge trough research in science, the arts and humanities and the dissemination of its results *(a)* The advancement of knowledge through **research** is an essential function of all **systems** of higher education, which should promote postgraduate studies. **Innovation, interdisciplinarity and transdisciplinarily** should be promoted and reinforced in programmes with long-term orientations on social and cultural aims and needs. An appropriate balance should be established between basic and target-oriented research.

(b) Institutions should ensure that all members of the academic community engaged in research are provided with appropriate training, resources and support. The intellectual and cultural rights on the results of research should be used to the benefit of humanity and should be protected so that they contact be abused.

(c) Research must be enhanced in all disciplines, including the social and human sciences, education (including higher education), engineering, natural sciences, mathematics, informatics and the arts within the framework of national, regional and international research and development policies. Of special importance is the enhancement of research capacities in higher education research institutions, as mutual enhancement of quality takes place when higher education and research are conducted at a higher level within the same institution. These institutions should find the material and financial support required, from **both public and private sources.**

Article 6. Long-term orientation based on relevance

(a) *Relevance* in higher education should be assessed in terms of the fit between what society expects of institutions and what they do. This requires ethical standards, political impartiality, critical capacities and, at the same time, a better articulation with the problems of society and the world of work, *basing*

long-term orientations on societal aims and needs, including respect for cultures and environmental protection. The concern is to provide access to both broad general education and targeted, career-specific education, often interdisciplinary, focusing on skills and aptitudes, both of which equip individuals to live in a variety of changing settings, and to be able to change occupations.

(b) Higher education should *reinforce its role of service to society,* especially its activities aimed at eliminating poverty, intolerance, violence, illiteracy, hunger, environmental degradation and disease, mainly through an *interdisciplinary and transdisciplinary approach* in the analysis of problems and issues.

(c) Higher education should enhance its contribution to *the development of the whole education system,* notably through improved teacher education, curriculum development and educational research.

(d) Ultimately, higher education should aim at the creation of a new society—non-violent and non-exploitative—consisting of highly cultivated, motivated and integrated individuals, inspired by love for humanity and guided by wisdom.

Article 7. Strengthening co-operation with the world of work and analysing and anticipating societal needs

(a) In economies characterised by changes and the emergence of new production paradigms based no knowledge and its application, and on the handling of information, the links between higher education, the world of work and other parts of society should be strengthened and renewed.

(b) Links with the world of work can be strengthened, through the participation of its representatives in the governance of institutions, the increased use of domestic and international apprenticeship/work-

study opportunities for students and teachers, the exchange of personnel between the world of work and higher education institutions and revised curricula more closely aligned with working practices.

(c) **As a lifelong source of professional training, updating and recycling,** institutions of higher education should systematically take into account trends in the world of work and in the scientific technological and economic sectors. In order to respond to the work requirements, higher education systems and the world of work should jointly develop and access learning processes, bridging programmes and prior learning assessment and recognition programmes, which integrate theory and training on the job. Within the framework of their anticipatory function, higher education institutions could contribute to the creation of new jobs, although that is not their only function.

(d) Developing entrepreneurial skills and initiative should become major concerns of higher education, in order to facilitate employability of graduates who will increasingly be called upon to be not only job seekers but also and above all to become job creators. Higher education institutions should give the opportunity to students to fully develop their own abilities with a sense of social responsibility, educating them to become full participants in democratic society and promoters of changes that will foster equity and justice.

Article 8. Diversification for enhanced equity of opportunity

(a) Diversifying higher education models and recruitment methods and criteria is essential both to meet increasing international demand and to provide access to various delivery modes and to extend access to an ever-wider public, in a lifelong

perspective, based on flexible entry and exit points to and from the system of higher education.

(b) More diversified systems of higher education are characterised by new types of tertiary institutions: public, private and non-profit institutions, amongst others. Institutions should be able to offer a wide variety of education and training opportunities: traditional degrees, short courses, part-time study, flexible schedules, modularised courses, supported learning at a distance, etc.

Article 9. Innovative educational approaches: critical thinking and creativity

(a) In a world undergoing rapid changes, there is a perceived need for a new vision and paradigm of higher education, which should be student-oriented, calling in most countries for in-depth reforms and an open access policy so as to cater for ever more diversified categories of people, and of its contents, methods, practices and means of delivery, based on new types of links and partnerships with the community and with the broadest sectors of society.

(b) Higher education institutions should educate students to become well informed and deeply motivated citizens, who can think critically, analyse problems of society, look for solutions to the problems of society, apply them and accept social responsibilities.

(c) To achieve these goals, it may be necessary to recast curricula, using new and appropriate methods, so as to go beyond cognitive mastery of disciplines. New pedagogical and didactical approaches should be accessible and promoted in order to facilitate the acquisition of skills, competences and abilities for communication, creative and critical analysis, **independent thinking and team work in multicultural contexts,** where creativity also involves combining traditional or local knowledge and

know-how with advanced science and technology. **These recast curricula should take into account the gender dimension and the specific cultural, historic and economic context of each country.** The teaching of human rights standards and education on the needs of communities in all parts of the world should be reflected in the curricula of all disciplines, particularly those preparing for entrepreneurship. Academic personnel should play a significant role in determining the curriculum.

(d) New methods of education will also imply new types of teaching-learning materials. These have to be coupled with new methods of testing that will promote not only powers of memory but also powers of comprehension, skills for practical work and creativity.

Article 10. Higher education personnel and students as major actors

(a) A vigorous policy of staff development is an essential element of higher education institutions. Clear policies should be established concerning higher education teachers, who nowadays need to focus on teaching students how to learn and how to take initiatives rather than being exclusively founts of knowledge. Adequate provision should be made for research and for updating and improving pedagogical skills, through appropriate staff development programmes, encouraging constant innovation in curriculum, teaching and learning methods, and ensuring appropriate professional and financial status, and **for excellence in research and teaching,** reflecting the corresponding provisions of the **Recommendation concerning the Status of Higher-Education Teaching Personnel approved by the General Conference of UNESCO in November 1997.** To this end, more importance should be attached to international experience. Furthermore, in view of the role of higher

education for lifelong learning, experience outside the institutions ought to be considered as a relevant qualification for higher educational staff.

(b) Clear policies should be established by all higher education institutions preparing teacher of early childhood education and for primary and secondary schools, providing stimulus for constant innovation in curriculum, best practices in teaching methods and familiarity with diverse learning styles. It is vital to have appropriately trained administrative and technical personnel.

(c) **National and institutional decision-makers should place students and their needs at the centre of their concerns,** and should consider them as major partners and responsible stakeholders in the renewal of higher education. This should include student involvement in issues that affect that level of education, in evaluation, the renovation of teaching methods and curricula and, in the institutional framework in force, in policy-formulation and institutional management. As students have the right to organize and represent themselves, students' involvement in these issues should be guaranteed.

(d) Guidance and counselling services should be developed, in co-operation with student organisations, in order to assist students in the transition to higher education at whatever age and to take account of the needs of ever more diversified categories of learners. Apart from those entering higher education from schools or further education colleges, they should also take account of the needs of those leaving and returning in a lifelong process. Such support is important in ensuring a good match between student and course, reducing dropout. Students who do drop out should have suitable opportunities to return to higher education if and when appropriate.

FROM VISION TO ACTION

Article 11. Qualitative evaluation

(a) **Quality in higher education is a multi-dimensional concept,** which should embrace all its functions, and activities: teaching and academic programmes, research and scholarship, staffing, students, buildings, facilities, equipment, services to the community and the academic environment. Internal self-evaluation and external review, conducted openly by independent specialists, if possible with international expertise, are vital for enhancing quality. Independent national bodies should be established and comparative standards of quality, recognised at international level, should be defined. **Due attention should be paid to specific institutional, national and regional contexts in order to take into account diversity and to avoid uniformity.** Stakeholders should be an integral part of the institutional evaluation process.

(b) Quality also requires that higher education should be characterised by its international dimension: exchange of knowledge, interactive networking, mobility of teachers and students and international research projects while taking into account the national cultural values and circumstances.

(c) To attain and sustain national regional or international quality, certain components are particularly relevant notably careful selection of staff and continuous staff development, in particular though the promotion of appropriate programmes for academic staff development, including teaching/learning methodology and mobility between countries, between higher education institutions, and between higher education institutions and the world of work, as well as student mobility within and between countries. The new information technologies are an important tool in this process, owing to their impact on the acquisition of knowledge and know-how.

Article 12. The potential and the challenge of technology

The rapid breakthroughs in new information and communication technologies will further change the way knowledge is developed, acquired and delivered. It is also important to note that the new technologies offer opportunities to innovate on course content and teaching methods and to widen access to higher learning. However, it should be borne in mind that new information technology does not reduce the need for teachers bout changes their role in relation to the learning process and that the continuous dialogue that converts information into knowledge and understanding becomes fundamental. Higher education institutions should lead in drawing on the advantages and potential of new information and communication technologies, ensuring quality and maintaining high standards for education practices and outcomes in a spirit of openness, equity and international cooperation by:

(a) engaging in networks, technology transfer, capacity-building, developing teaching meaterials and sharing experience of their application in teaching, training and research, making knowledge accessible to all;

(b) creating new learning environments, ranging from distance education facilities to complete virtual higher education institutions and systems, capable of bridging distances and developing high-quality systems of education, thus serving social and economic advancement and democratisation as well as other relevant priorities of society, while ensuring that these virtual education facilities, based on regional, continental or global networks, function in a way that respects cultural and social identities;

(c) noting that, in making full use of information and communication technology (ICT) for educational purposes, particular attention should be paid to removing and grave inequalities which exist among and also within the countries of the world with regard to access to new information and

communication technologies and to the production of the corresponding resources;

(d) adapting ICT to national, regional and local needs and securing technical, educational, management and institutional systems to sustain it;

(e) facilitating, through international co-operation, the identification of the objectives and interests of all countries, particularly the developing countries, equitable access and the strengthening of infrastructures in this field and the dissemination of such technology throughout society;

(f) closely following the evolution of the 'knowledge society' in order to ensure high quality and equitable regulations for access to prevail;

(g) taking the new possibilities created by the use of ICTs into account, while realising that it is, above all, institutions of higher education that are using ICTs in order to modernize their work, and not ICTs transforming institutions of higher education from real to virtual institutions.

Article 13. Strengthening higher education management and financing

(a) The management and financing of higher education require the **development of appropriate planning and policy-analysis capacities** and strategies, based on partnerships established between higher education institutions and state and national planning and co-ordination bodies, so as to secure appropriately streamlined management and the cost-effective use of resources. Higher education institutions should **adopt forward-looking management practices** that respond to the needs of their environments. Managers in higher education must be responsive, competent and able to evaluate regularly, by internal and extent mechanisms, the effectiveness of procedures and administrative rules.

(*b*) Higher education institutions must be given autonomy to manage their internal affairs, but with this autonomy must come clear and transparent accountability to the government, parliament, students and the wider society.

(*c*) The ultimate goal of management should be to enhance the institutional mission by ensuring high-quality teaching, training and research, and services to the community. This objective requires **governance that combines social vision, including understanding of global issues, with efficient managerial skills.** Leadership in higher education is thus a major social responsibility and can be significantly strengthened through dialogue with all stakeholders, especially teachers and students, in higher education. The participation of teaching faculty in the governing bodies of higher education institutions should be taken into account, within the framework of current institutional arrangements, bearing in mind the need to keep the size of these bodies within reasonable bounds.

(*d*) The promotion of North-South co-operation to ensure the necessary financing for strengthening higher education in the developing countries is essential.

Article 14. Financing of higher education as a public service

The funding of higher education requires both public and private resources. The role of the state remains essential in this regard.

(*a*) The diversification of funding sources reflects the support that society provides to higher education and must be further strengthened to ensure the development of higher education, increase its efficiency and maintain its quality and relevance. **Public support for higher education and research remains essential** to ensure a balanced achievement of educational and social missions.

(*b*) Society as a whole must support education at all levels, including higher education, given its role in promoting sustainable economic, social and cultural development. **Mobilisation for this purpose depends on public awareness and involvement of the public and private sectors** of the economy, parliaments, the media, governmental and non-governmental organisations, students as well as institutions, families and all the social actors involved with higher education.

Article 15. Sharing knowledge and know-how across borders and continents

(*a*) The principle of solidarity and true partnerships amongst higher education institutions worldwide is crucial for education and training in all fields that encourage an understanding of global issues, the role of democratic governance and skilled human resources in their resolution, and the need for living together with different cultures and values. The practice of multilingualism, faculty and student exchange programmes and institutional linkage to promote intellectual and scientific co-operation should be an integral part of all higher education systems.

(*b*) The principles if international co-operation based on solidarity, recognition and mutual support, true partnership that equitably services the interests of the partners and the value of sharing knowledge and know-how across borders should govern relationships among higher education institutions in both developed and developing countries and should benefit the least developed countries in particular. Consideration should be given to the need for safeguarding higher education institutional capacities in regions suffering from conflict or natural disasters. Consequently, an international dimension should permeate the curriculum, and the teaching and learning processes.

(c) Regional and international normative instruments for the recognition of studies should be ratified and implemented, including certification of the skills, competences and abilities of graduates, making it easier for students to change courses, in order to facilitate mobility within and between national systems.

Article 16. From 'brain drain' to 'brain gain'

The 'brain drain' has yet to be stemmed, since it continues to deprive that developing countries and those in transition, of the high-level expertise necessary to accelerate their socio-economic progress. International co-operation schemes should be based on long-term partnerships between institutions in the South and the North, and also promote South-South co-operation. Priority should be given to training programmes in the developing countries, in centres of excellence forming regional and international networks, with short periods of specialised and intensive study abroad. Consideration should be given to creating an environment conducive to attracting and retaining skilled human capital, either through national policies or international arrangements to facilitate the return—permanent or temporary—of highly trained scholars and researchers to their countries of origin. At the same time, efforts must be directed towards a process of 'brain gain' through collaboration programmes that, by virtue of their international dimension, enhance the building and strengthening of institutions and facilitate full use of endogenous capacities. Experience gained through the UNITWIN/UNESCO Chairs Programme and the principles enshrined in the regional conventions on the recognition of degrees and diplomas in higher education are of particular importance in this respect.

Article 17. Partnership and alliances

Partnership and alliances amongst stakeholders—national and institutional policy—makers, teaching and **related** staff, researchers and students, and administrative and technical personnel in institutions of higher education, the world of work, community groups-is a powerful force in managing change. Also, non-governmental organisations are key actors in this process. Henceforth, **partnership, based on common interest, mutual respect and credibility, should be a prime matrix for renewal in higher education.**

We, the participants in the World Conference on Higher Education, adopt this Declaration and reaffirm the right of all people to education and the right of access to higher education based on individual merit and capacity;

We pledge to act together within the frame of our individual and collective responsibilities, by taking all necessary measures in order to realize the principles concerning higher education contained in the Universal Declaration of Human Rights and in the Convention against Discrimination in Education;

We solemnly reaffirm our commitment to peace. To that end, we are determined to accord high priority to education for peace and to participate in the celebration of the International Year for the Culture of Peace in the year 2000;

We adopt, therefore, this World Declaration on Higher Education for the Twenty-First Century: Vision and Action. To achieve the goals set fourth in this Declaration and, in particular, for immediate action, we agree on the following Framework for Priority Action for Change and Development Higher Education.

(adopted by the World Conference on Higher Education on 9 October 1998).

3

Framework for Priority Action for Change and Development of Higher Education

I. Priority Actions at National Level

1. **States, including their governments, parliaments and other decision-makers,** should:

   (a) establish, where appropriate, the legislative, political and financial framework for the reform and further development of higher education, in keeping with the terms of the Universal Declaration of Human Rights, which establishes that **higher education shall be 'accessible to all on the basis of merit'. No discrimination can be accepted,** no one can be excluded from higher education or its study fields, degree levels and types of institutions on grounds of race, gender, language, religion, or age or because of any economic or social distinctions or physical disabilities;

   (b) reinforce the links between higher education and research;

   (c) consider and use higher education as a catalyst for the entire education system;

   (d) develop higher education institutions to include lifelong learning approaches, giving learners an

optimal range of choice and a flexibility of entry and exit points within the system, and redefine their role accordingly, which implies the development of open and continuous access to higher learning and the need for bridging programmes and prior learning assessment and recognition;

(e) make efforts, when necessary, to establish close links between higher education and research institutions, taking into account the fact that education and research are two closely related elements in the establishment of knowledge;

(f) develop innovative schemes of collaboration between institutions of higher education and different sectors of society to ensure that higher education and research programmes affectively contribute to local, regional and national development;

(g) fulfil their commitments to higher education and be accountable for the pledges adopted with their concurrence, at several forums, particularly over the past decade, with regard to human, material and financial resources, human development and education in general, and to higher education in particular;

(h) have a policy framework to ensure new partnerships and the involvement of all relevant stakeholders in all aspects of higher education: the evaluation process, including curriculum and pedagogical renewal, and guidance and counselling services; and, in the framework of existing institutional arrangements, policy-making and institutional governance;

(i) **define and implement policies to eliminate all gender stereotyping in higher education** and to consolidate women's participation at all levels and in all disciplines in which they are under-represented at present and, it particular, to enhance their active involvement in decision-making;

(j) **establish clear policies concerning higher education teachers,** as set out in the Recommendation concerning the Status of Higher-Education Teaching Personnel approved by the General Conference of UNESCO in November 1997;

(k) recognize students as the centre of attention of higher education, and one of its stakeholders. They should be involved, by means of adequate institutional structures, in the renewal of their level of education (including curriculum and pedagogical reform), and policy decision, in the framework of existing institutional arrangements;

(l) recognize that students have the right to organize themselves autonomously;

(m) promote and facilitate national and international mobility of teaching staff and students as an essential part of the quality and relevance of higher education;

(n) provide and ensure those conditions necessary for the exercise of academic freedom and institutional autonomy so as to allow institutions of higher education, as well as those individuals engaged in higher education and research, to fulfil their obligations to society.

2. States in which enrolment in higher education is low by internationally accepted comparative standards should strive to ensure a level of higher education adequate for relevant needs in the public and private sectors of society and to establish plans for diversifying and expanding access, particularly benefiting all minorities and disadvantaged groups.

3. The interface with general, technical and professional secondary education should be reviewed in depth, in the context of lifelong learning. Access to higher education in whatever form must remain open to those successfully completing secondary education or its equivalent or meeting entry qualifications at any age, while creating

gateways to higher education, especially for older students without any formal secondary education certificates, by attaching more importance to their professional experience. However, **preparation for higher education should not be the sole or primary purpose of secondary education, which should also prepare for the world of work,** with complementary training whenever required, in order to provide knowledge, capacities and skills for a wide range of jobs. The concept of bridging programmes should be promoted to allow those entering the job market to return to studies at a later date.

4. **Concrete steps should be taken to reduce the widening gap between industrially developed and developing countries, in particular the least developed countries, with regard to higher education and research.** Concrete steps are also needed to encourage increased co-operation between countries at all levels of economic development with regard to higher education and research. Consideration should be given to making budgetary provisions for that purpose, and developing mutually beneficial agreements involving industry, national as well as international, in order to sustain co-operative activities and projects through appropriate incentives and funding in education, research and the development of high-level experts in these countries.

II. Priority Actions at the Level of Systems and Institutions

5. **Each higher education institution should define its mission according to the present and future needs of society** and base it on an awareness of the fact that higher education is essential for any country or region to reach and necessary level of sustainable and environmentally sound economic and social development, cultural creativity nourished by better knowledge and understanding of the cultural heritage, higher living standards, and internal and international harmony and

peace, based on human rights, democracy, tolerance and mutual respect. These missions should incorporate the concept of academic freedom set out in the Recommendation concerning the Status of Higher-Education Teaching Personnel approved by the General Conference of UNESCO in November 1997.

6. In establishing priorities in their programmes and structures, higher education institutions should:

   (a) take into account the need to abide by the rules of ethics and scientific and intellectual rigour, and the multidisciplinary and transdisciplinary approach;

   (b) be primarily concerned to establish systems of access for the benefit of all persons who have the necessary abilities and motivations;

   (c) use their autonomy and higher academic standards to contribute to the sustainable development of society and to the resolution of the issues facing the society of the future. They should develop their capacity to give forewarning through the analysis of emerging social, cultural, economic and political trends, approached in a multidisciplinary and transdisciplinary manner, giving particular attention to:

   - high quality, a clear sense of the social pertinence of studies and their anticipatory function, based n scientific grounds;
   - knowledge of fundamental social questions, in particular related to the elimination of poverty, to sustainable development, to intercultural dialogue and to the shaping of a culture of peace;
   - the need for close connection with effective research organisations or institutions that perform well in the sphere of research;
   - the development of the whole education system in the perspective of the recommendations and

the new goals for education as set out in the 1996 report to UNESCO of the International Commission on Education for the Twenty-first Century;

- fundamentals of human ethics, applied to each profession and to all areas of human endeavour;

(d) ensure, especially in universities and as far as possible, that faculty members participate in teaching, research, tutoring students and steering institutional affairs;

(e) take all necessary measures to reinforce their service to the community, especially their activities aimed at eliminating poverty, intolerance, violence, illiteracy, hunger and disease, through an interdisciplinary and transdisciplinary approach in the analysis of challenges, problems and different subjects;

(f) **set their relations with the world of work on a new basis** involving effective partnerships with all social actors concerned, starting from a reciprocal harmonisation of action and the search for solutions to pressing problems of humanity, all this within a framework of responsible autonomy and academic freedoms;

(g) ensure high quality of international standing, **consider accountability** and both internal and external evaluation, with due respect for autonomy and academic freedom, **as being normal and inherent in their functioning,** and institutionalize transparent systems, structures of mechanisms special thereto;

(h) as lifelong education requires academic staff to update and improve their teaching skills and learning methods, even more than in the present systems mainly based on short periods of higher teaching, establish appropriate academic staff development structures and/or mechanisms and programmes;

(i) **promote and develop research, which is a necessary feature of all higher education systems,** in all disciplines, including the human and social sciences and arts, given their relevance for development. Also, research on higher education itself should be strengthened through mechanisms such as the UNESCO/UNU Forum on Higher Education and the UNESCO Chairs in Higher Education. Objective, timely studies are needed to ensure continued progress towards such key national objectives as access, equity, quality relevance and diversification;

(j) remove **gender inequalities and biases in curricula and research,** and take all appropriate measures to ensure balanced representation of both men and women among students and teachers, at all levels of management;

(k) **provide,** where appropriate, **guidance and counselling, remedial courses, training in how to study and other forms of students support,** including measures to improve student living condition.

7. While the need for closer links between higher education and the world of work is important worldwide, it is particularly vital for the developing countries and especially the least developed countries, given their low level of economic development. Governments of these countries should take appropriate measures to reach this objective through appropriate measures such as strengthening institutions of higher/professional/vocational education. At the same time, international action is needed in order to help establish joint undertakings between higher education and industry in these countries. It will be necessary to give consideration to ways in which higher education graduates could be supported, through various schemes, following the positive experience of the micro-credit system and other incentives, in order to start small - and medium-size enterprises. At the institutional

level, developing entrepreneurial skills and initiative should become a major concern of higher education, in order to facilitate employability of graduates who will increasingly be required not only to be job-seekers but to become job-creators.

8. **The use of new technologies should be generalised to the greatest extent possible** to help higher education institutions, to reinforce academic development, to widen access, to attain universal scope and to extend knowledge, as well as to facilitate education throughout life. Governments, educational institutions and the private sector should ensure that informatics and communication network infrastructures, computer facilities and human resources training are adequately provided.

9. **Institutions of higher education should be open to adult learners:**

   (a) by developing coherent mechanisms to recognize the outcomes of learning undertaken in different contexts, and to ensure that credit is transferable within and between institutions, sectors and states;

   (b) by establishing joint higher education/community research and training partnerships, and by bringing the services of higher education institutions to outside groups;

   (c) by carrying out interdisciplinary research in all aspects of adult education and learning with the participation of adult learners themselves;

   (d) by creating opportunities for adult learning in flexible, open and creative ways.

III. Actions to be Taken at International Level and, in Particular, to be Initiated by UNESCO

10. **Co-operation should be conceived of as an integral part of the institutional missions of higher education institutions and systems.** Intergovernmental organisations, donor agencies and non-governmental

organisations should extend their action in order to develop inter-university co-operation projects in particular through twining institutions, based on solidarity and partnership, as a means of bridging the gap between rich and poor countries in the vital areas of knowledge production and application. Each institution of higher education should envisage the creation of an appropriate structure and/or mechanism for promoting and managing international co-operation.

11. UNESCO, and other intergovernmental organisations and non-governmental organisations active in higher education, the states through their bilateral and multilateral co-operation programmes, the academic community and all concerned partners in society should further **promote international academic mobility** as a means to advance knowledge and knowledge-sharing in order to bring about and promote solidarity as a main element of the global knowledge society of tomorrow, including through strong support for the joint work plan (1999-2005) of the six intergovernmental committees in charge of the application of the regional conventions on the recognition of studies, degrees and diplomas in higher education and through large-scale co-operative action involving, *inter alia,* the establishment of an educational credit transfer scheme, with particular emphasis on South-South co-operation, the needs of the least developed countries and of the states with few higher education institutions or none at all.

12. Institutions of higher education in industrialised countries should strive to make arrangements for international co-operation with sister institutions in developing countries and in particular with those of poor countries. In their co-operation, the institutions should make efforts to ensure fair and just recognition of studies abroad. UNESCO should take initiatives to develop higher education throughout the world, setting itself clear-cut goals that could lead to tangible results. One method

might be to implement projects in different regions renewing efforts towards creating and/or strengthening centres of excellence in developing countries, in particular through the UNITWIN/UNESCO Chairs Programme, relying on networks of national, regional and international higher education institutions.

13. UNESCO, together with all concerned parts of society, should also undertake action in order to **alleviate the negative effects of 'brain drain' and to shift to a dynamic process of 'brain gain'.** An overall analysis is required in all regions of the world of the causes and effects of brain drain. **A vigorous campaign** should be launched **through the concerted effort of the international community** and on the basis of academic solidarity and should encourage the return to their home country of expatriate academics, as well as the involvement of **university volunteers**—newly retired academics or young academics at the beginning of their career-who wish to teach and undertake research at higher education institutions in developing countries. At the same time it is essential to support the developing countries in their efforts to build and strengthen their own educational capacities.

14. Within this framework, UNESCO should:

    (a) **promote better co-ordination among inter-governmental, supranational and non-governmental organisations, agencies and foundations that sponsor existing programmes and projects of international co-operation in higher education.** Furthermore, co-ordination efforts should take place in the context of national priorities. This could be conducive to the pooling and sharing of resources, avoid overlapping and promote better identification of projects, greater impact of action and increased assurance of their validity through collective agreement and review. Programmes aiming at the rapid transfer of knowledge, supporting institutional

development and establishing centres of excellence in all areas of knowledge, in particular for peace education, conflict resolution, human rights and democracy, should be supported by institutions and by public and private donors;

(b) jointly with the United Nations University and with National Commissions and various intergovernmental and non-governmental organisations, become a forum of reflection on higher education issues aiming at: (i) preparing update reports on the state of knowledge on higher education issues in all parts of the world; (ii) promoting innovative projects of training and research, intended to enhance the specific role of higher education in lifelong education; (iii) reinforcing international co-operation and emphasising the role of higher education for citizenship education, sustainable development and peace; and (iv) facilitating exchange of information and establishing, when appropriate, a database on successful experiences and innovations that can be consulted by institutions confronted worth problems in their reforms of higher education;

(c) take specific action to support institutions of higher education in the lest developed parts of the world and in regions suffering the effects of conflict or natural disasters;

(d) make renewed efforts towards creating or/and strengthening centres of excellence in developing countries;

(e) take the initiative to draw up an international instrument on academic freedom, autonomy and social responsibility in connection with the Recommendation concerning the Status of Higher-Education Teaching Personnel;

(f) ensure follow-up to the World Declaration on Higher Education and the Framework for Priority Action, jointly with other intergovernmental and non-governmental organisations and with all higher

education stakeholders, including the United Nations University, the NGO Collective Consultation on Higher Education and the UNESCO Student Forum. It should have a crucial role in promoting international co-operation in the field of higher education in implementing this follow-up. Consideration should be given to according priority to this in the development of UNESCO's next draft Programme and Budget.

(adopted by the World Conference on Higher Education on 9 October 1998).

Part II

Regional Declarations and Action Plans

4

Africa

Declaration and Action Plan on Higher Education in Africa

We, participants at the **African Regional Consultation** preparatory to the World Conference on Higher Education,[1]

1. **Recalling** the Universal Declaration of Human Rights, article 26, of which affirms that, 'Everyone has the right to education'... and that 'higher education shall be accessible to all, on the basis of merit', and further recalling the Convention Against Discrimination in the field of Education, adopted by UNESCO in 1960, which calls on Member States to 'make higher education accessible to all, based on individual abilities';
2. **Taking into account** UNESCO's Constitution, which encourages inter-institutional exchanges in the field of Education;
3. **Adhering to** the conclusions and recommendations of the *Policy Paper on Change and Development in Higher Education* published by UNESCO in 1995, as well as the major conclusions of the International Commission on Education for the Twenty-first Century, which stipulate that, 'Universities in developing countries have a duty to carry out research that should contribute to solving the most serious problems facing these countries';

1. Dakar, Senegal, 1-4 April 1997.

4. **Taking into account** the desire of the United Nations to improve co-ordination of the actions of organisations of the United Nations system in order to reinforce their impact on the development of the Africa region, by mobilising every effort in the same vein as the creation of an Africa Department by UNESCO) and allocating necessary funds for in-depth reform of higher education in Africa;

5. **Having taken note of** the conclusions of the Priority Africa seminars on Higher Education in Africa (Accra: November 1991; Dakar: November 1992; Alexandria: April 1993) *summary papers* (such as *Higher Education in Africa: Trends and Challenges for the 21st Century*. Dakar 1992 and publications life *Future Directions for Higher Education in Africa* published by BREDA in 1994 and *Audience of Africa. Social Development. Priorities for Africa, Final Report (1995)* and taken further into account the findings of the Second World Congress on and Education and Informatics organised by UNESCO in Moscow in July 1996, and other reports by various international and African institutions which have also carried our diagnosis and developed guidelines for action;

6. **Observing** that significant but not quite remarkable progress has been made in Africa through the efforts of higher education institutions to wit: progress in implementing democratic structures, improved access to higher education, training of senior management level personnel for the public and the private sectors, development of programmes of African studies, rediscovery and promotion of the historical and cultural heritage, etc.;

7. **Recognising** at the same time, the persistence of problems needing urgent solutions (e.g.) poverty, hunger, disease, unemployment, illiteracy, the debt burden, unfavorable trading conditions, inflection, all forms and types of conflicts, environmental degradation, etc.);

8. **Observing** that Africa is more seriously affected than the other regions of the world by the deep-seated societal changes of our time, viz:

- the upsurge of economic liberalism, globalisation, and the prevailing world order which serves the interests of the strongest economic and financial powers, deregulation the African market, the rise of an uncontrolled and perhaps uncontrollable underground economy;
- outsourcing, which is of little benefit to Africa, in view of the trend for fund managers to associate Africa with political instability and an insufficient of qualified and skilled persons;
- structural adjustment policies leading to loss of jobs in the public sector, (loses not fully absorbed by the private sector) and which have tended to devalue the degress awarded by institutions of higher education;
- and upward demographic surge which has tended to increase the demand for education, uncontrolled urban and an population growth;
- displaced populations, the result of economic difficulties or the trauma of wars—a situation difficult to manage by the countries receiving such displaced persons;
- exponential growth in knowledge, with very little direct contribution from the Africa region;
- rapid development of new information and communications technologies, with the risk of widening the gap between Africa and the other regions of the world;

9. **Pointing out** that the challenges facing the Africa region and the sweeping changes in society make the structural problems of higher educational institutions all the more critical.

   The problems include:

   - coping with surging numbers of students in the face of declining budgets;
   - excessively high student/teacher ratios, which make individual attention to learners difficult;

- undue attention to municipal and social services, which reduces funds available for teaching and research;
- deterioration of infrastructure, due to lack of maintenance;
- insufficient remuneration of academics, leading to loss of motivation, moonlighting and brain drain;
- imbalance in students enrolments between science and technology based programmes and the humanities;
- gender inequity at all levels: within the student body, within academic staff, and within the decision-making cadre;
- insufficient attention to, and the insufficient resources for research;
- lack of a long-term vision in the planning and management of teaching and research activities;
- insufficient pedagogical training of teachers in higher education, coupled with a lack of systematic management training for institutional and system-wide managers;
- teaching-learning procedures often in the form of memorisation and to the neglect of inculcating the analytical and problem solving skills needed for tackling societal problems.

10. **What is therefore needed** is the development of new guidelines focusing on the following key issues: relevance, quality, management/finance, and co-operation.

11. **Relevance** is the number one problem, for, should African higher education institutions and the authorities responsible for them interpret their missions wrongly, they will not be able to take up the above challenges: the institutions could in fact become obstacles to development. First of all, it *is imperative that they adapt their missions of the needs and constraints of the local, national, regional, and international environments.* This is one of

those external efficiency indicators by which institutions are judged. This entails links with the 'town': promoters of economic activities and all groups and persons working to ensure the reign of equity and better living conditions for Africans, those engaged in promoting responsible citizenship and ensuring a culture of peace and sustainable human development.

Relevance also requires better articulation with the world of work and with other efforts geared towards improving the contribution of higher education to the entire educational system, especially through teacher training and research in education.

12. **Quality** is the second area needing thought and action. It is closely linked to the issue of relevance but entails the operationalisation of the envisaged outcomes (a clear definition of goals and objectives) of the inputs the institutions will work with (thus a review of admissions criteria) and the processes and procedures for working with the inputs (the way the management system coordinates structures, resources and the institutional culture to obtain the required products). *A policy of total quality can* be implemented through comparisons between observed and intended outcomes (in terms of quantitative and qualitative internal efficiency) and constant analysis of the sources of dysfunction. This will require a culture of *Autonomy* for higher education institutions as well as of their constituent units. It will also require careful attention to the problems of students and teachers and solidarity and responsibility towards the institution as a project for promoting local development and for ensuring a take-off for national and regional development. Thus the need for *accountability,* which is indissociable from the concept of quality.

13. **Management and Funding** constitute the third major concern. An institution could undertake an in-depth analysis on its mission and translate this into product, process and quality indicators. If however, the institution fails to built quality into its entire modus operandi, and

if financial resources are inadequate, if is likely to achieve very little and so very unlikely to be able to meet the challenges of Africa's development. We would therefore urge that higher institutions accept the imperative of adopting *forward-looking management* practices which respond to the needs of the environment, as specified in their missions.

14. **Co-operation** at the national, regional and international levels is the fourth key issue. Co-operation projects have often been mere juxtaposition of disparate efforts not sufficiently linked to an *overall strategic plan,* specifying priorities, deadlines and the constraints arising from the relationships between various projects or components of projects. We would expect that the organisation of African institutions into co-operative *networks*, using appropriate products of new technologies, should be a major priority area.

15. **On basis of these observations** we would suggest the following areas of concrete action:

To Improve Relevance

16. We recommend that Member States *develop educational programmes* capable of meeting the challenges of sweeping societal changes and the principal challenges which Africa is bound to face in the immediate future.

17. We would suggest that *Member States create 'observatories' to monitor changes in the employment market,* of imminent social changes, of new approaches to research and development-related activities. Such observatories would help the process of developing national educational plan, as data would be made available to institutions of higher learning, to improve their capacity to align their missions with national priority areas.

18. We would suggest that national education programmes aim at *diversification* with a greater emphasis on a *regionalisation* of specific disciplines. This could be a means of getting institutions to serve the specific needs

of disadvantages areas and groups. These programmes should target specific needs that will generate employment or create jobs; training programmes and structures should be flexible in order to adapt rapidly to changing needs. It would also be necessary to develop (in consultation with appropriate stakeholders) a wider variety of short duration programmes.

19. We feel that appropriate steps ought to be taken to convince Member States that investment in institutions of higher education is worthwhile, as long as the institutions are oriented to meet the needs of society. International organisations like UNESCO will have to make strong moves to sensitise top political and financial authorities on this issue.

20. Institutions of higher education should define their mission statements in the form of overall general guidelines. These should be closely linked with the national education programmes and based on a thorough analysis of needs, in co-operation with the institution's internal and external actors. They should be presented in the form of observable outcomes.

21. It would be more profitable to define educational programmes henceforth in terms of expected outcomes, and not simply in terms of facts to be transmitted and reproduced, or in terms of mere course titles. This will contribute to the evolution of genuine education programmes with special emphasis on analysis of complex situations, teamwork, higher cognitive skills, the inculcation of responsible citizenship and the development of a culture of peace.

22. Institutions of higher education should make special efforts to develop *scientific and technological programmes* to help meet the demands of the accelerated development of new technologies, especially new information and communication technologies. These programmes should be supported by intensive research activities, from which the critical mass of the expertise needed for the region's development as it faces the pressures of globalisation. We

suggest that institutions already have expertise in these areas create a network, with the assistance of UNESCO and other organisations.

Existing potentials on information and communications technologies should be boosted to give rise to *virtual universities,* which could considerably improve access, while at the same time providing world-class educational resources.

23. Higher education institutions should also make special efforts to promote integrated programmes aimed at seeking appropriate *solutions to the major problems of the progressive evolution* of a culture of peace and promotion of sustainable development oriented towards reducing hunger and protecting the environment. Such programmes should build on the fruits of social research and designed to the promotion of research, the strengthening of expertise and consultancy services.

24. We recommend that research be made to bear a closer relation to the needs of African societies, *so that basic research can be more closely linked with applied and development-oriented research* stressing genuine partnerships with public and private institutions and the civil society. This would be one way of ensuring the active involvement of higher institutions in societal development efforts.

25. We recommend that *higher degree programmes* be organised around a qualitative and qualitative critical mass of committed academics, working together in a qualitatively conductive environment on subjects relevant to Africa's development. Doctoral training programmes can be restructured using team work or networking strategies.

26. We would like to stress the importance and urgency of carrying *out a series of case studies on Africa's priorities,* in which higher education institutions should play an important role. These include: the types of leadership to be promoted, strategic management and planning, systemic interactions between primary, secondary, tertiary and

continuing education, revision of programmes of education and training, the relative importance and feasibility of face-to-face and distance teaching programmes, strategies for ensuring improved participation of women in education and in decision making bodies, town and country planning, measures against the security problems of Africa (such as poverty, displaced populations, the trauma of war...). The Association of African Universities could undertake this task, with the assistance support of UNESCO and the possible collaboration of other organisations working in the field of higher education in Africa.

27. To become more responsive to the needs of society, and in order to acquire greater financial autonomy, we recommend that higher education institutions create structures for the development and management of consultancy activities, which are an essential part of their missions. For this to happen higher institutions should develop an entrepreneurial spirit as a means of strengthening their service functions which are in themselves complementary to their teaching and research functions.

28. We recommend that Member States organize regional conferences of ministers in charge of higher education, heads of institutions, and organisations or associations involved in the development of higher education.

To Improve the Quality

29. We recommend that each Member State establish a mechanism for *evaluating the quality* of higher education institutions, building on existing practices in the region. Such a body will be responsible for evaluating training, research and consultancy activities in the light of institutional missions national education programmes and the needs of changing times. *This should be a control rather than a punitive mechanism,* and should use a combination of internal and external evaluation strategies.

30. In order to ensure the quality of programmes, institutions of higher education will required to *establish minimum teaching-learning guidelines for each course module.* The

should explicitly state learners, entry and exist behaviours in terms of skills, values and attitudes, the teaching and evaluation methods, all within a specific time frame. They will constitute a point of reference and a form of moral contract between various internal and external actors.

31. It would be necessary for every institution to develop, a *data base on the quantitative and qualitative movement of students.* This data base should include any information that could be used to evaluate internal (and even external) efficiency, as well as trends in progress or non-progress in terms of the equity of the system. The data base should provide decision-makers at various levels with the information needed for the development of a *total quality policy,* or with the involvement of all stakeholders.

32. We expect that, with assistance from UNESCO and other regional or international organisations, every higher education institution will *establish a teaching-learning resource unit* staffed by skilled personnel charged with the task of pedagogical skill development and other forms of teaching-support activities.

33. We also hope that every institution will create appropriate structures for valuating and controlling the quality of its curricula (including the performance of students), in keeping with agreed guidelines.

34. We recommend that UNESCO call on Member Stats to improve the living and working conditions and emoluments of academics and, more importantly, to guarantee the autonomy of higher education.

35. We declare our support for the project on the conditions and status of higher education personnel, recently approved by an international committee of intergovernmental experts and which will be at the 29th General Conference of UNESCO (Paris, November 1997).

36. Having observed the undesirable effects of conflicts and strikes in universities, we suggest that institutions should create an enabling climate for dialogue with a strong emphasis *on prevention rather than repression.*

37. Convinced that research (as a fundamental mission of higher institutions) will need to be reinforced, we call for a substantial increase in the number of *academic journal* and the implementation of a coherent publications policy at sub-regional and regional levels. UNESCO could call on the organisations which took part in the present Consultation to submit concrete proposals on this issue.

38. Efforts to improve quality in each institution will be facilitated it Member States could develop *regional networks* for education and training activities as well as for research and consultancy activities. We call on UNESCO to lend its full weight to such networks.

39. We suggest that, at the regional level, existing institutions and organisations (such as CAMES for example) whose aim is to *harmonise qualifications and certification procedures* be strengthened, so that the potential for mobility is increased for both students and teachers, in line with the practice in other regions.

To Improve Management and Funding

40. We suggest that Member States guarantee equal rights to higher education based on ability and aptitude (i.e. merit). Member States *should take on principal responsibility for funding for higher education.* However, since it will be difficult for Member States to bear the entire financial burden, additional sources should be sought using the political and administrative mechanism of each State, whose sovereignty should be respected. We strongly advice that the economic conditions of families be taken into consideration, and that the only criteria for access or non-access should be merit.

41. To improve efficiency and strengthen the management of higher education institutions, it would be necessary to develop appropriate mechanism for regular dialogue between the institutions and their partners, particularly State structures, without compromising the autonomy of the institutions.

42. It is important to build the habit of *forward-looking management and planning* into higher education

institutions in Africa. This means that appropriate training opportunities should be provided for administrators, whether they occupy a permanent or an elected position. It also means that necessary computer database should be developed as soon as possible to ensure high-quality forward-looking management and planning. The institutions should find either within themselves or through co-operation the necessary skills to create, maintain and develop these data banks. UNESCO should seek support from organisations such as the Association of African Universities, the International Institute of Educational Planning, the Association of Commonwealth Universities, the Commonwealth Secretariat, etc., in this aspect of its work. The goal is for, African universities could be managed like high-performance service businesses able to play a crucial role in solving the problems besetting the Africa region.

43. We believe quality management is not the sole responsibility of top academic authorities. Each sub-system (faculty, department or other structures) should also take on responsibility for forward-looking management and planning. This means that each unit must clearly define its missions to bring them in line with the overall mission of the institution, translate them into observable indicators, and allocate the resource available in accordance with the mission and with a clear order or priority. They should also prepare regular activity reports, which they should be shared with staff and supervising authorities. This mode of management entails a certain degree of autonomy (thus a margin for manoeuvre) and full commitment to institutional goals. *The culture of evaluation and responsibility* must therefore be strengthened, or established in those institutions that still practice the rigid centralisation inherited from certain colonial structures.

44. We feel that, despite the prevailing financial crisis, the management of higher education institutions cannot be reduced to financial management based on purely

economic criteria. One should take in account *some criterion of equity* (such as women's or underprivileged persons' access to higher education) and *the criterion of social relevance* applied to teaching, research and consultancy activities. We would expect each institution's activity reports to include actions taken towards this end and the results obtained, in order to promote awareness in the appropriate ministerial authorities and obtain recognition and support for relevant actions.

45. Since WOMEN have a major role to play in the development of the Africa region, we request that international organisations, Member States and higher education institutions *develop well-articulated policies,* remove gender inequity in education and more importantly promote the advancement of women in the entire society. This should include measures implemented, by the institutions of higher education themselves. We suggest that meaningful *affirmative action be taken* in all possible directions. Women's associations and networks should be fully supported. A systematic and coherent policy of gender research and cases studies should be implemented and their findings widely publicised and ploughed back into the teaching, management and overall development work of higher education institutions.

46. We recommend that measures be taken to double the number of women (students, teachers and decision-makers) in higher education, within the next ten years. *Particular attention should be paid to orienting women towards scientific and technological disciplines.*

47. *We consider that student involvement in decision-making bodies should be given a considerable boost, with greater attention paid to their needs by taking into consideration students' perspectives which are often relevant to the analyses of problems and to the search for viable solutions. Student involvement is also equally a means of inculcating the leadership skills needed in after-school life as workers and as citizens.*

48. *At the regional level, it would be necessary to organize regular meetings under the aegis of organs like the Association of African Universities, for exchange on problems related to the management and funding of institutions of higher education. These meetings should be used to improve the operation of the institutons themselves and to develop the capacity for meaningful pressure on ministerial authorities in charge of higher education. The authorities should themselves be involved in these meetings.*

49. *We would suggest that, at the regional level, a student association forum be organised as a means of mobilising students to contribute to current efforts aimed at making higher education institutions more forceful, more active and more efficient partners, in the promotion of sustainable development in Africa. The conclusions of the forum could form Africa's contribution to the International Students' Forum to be held in Paris in 1998, as part of the commemoration of the fiftieth anniversary of the Declaration on Human Rights and the World Conference on Higher Education.*

To Reinforce Co-operation

50. We invite existing associations of institutions and of subject specialists as well as national, regional and international organisations to *support and* co-ordinate actions and projects aimed at establishing or strengthening inter-African and intercontinental networks working to reduce the gap between Africa and other regions by solving key regional development problems. Institutions of higher education should adopt a proactive policy in this connection and invest all their energy into fighting poverty, environmental degradation, discrimination of all kinds, and the ravages of conflicts.

51. We recommend that institutions of higher learning *create networks* of *centres of excellence* responding to the most pressing needs of the African continent, in terms to training, research and consultancy. Each institution should focus on

an area of expertise in which it is likely to excel, as its contribution to a regional skill–sharing network. Such strategies of solidarity/complementarity could enable Africa to meet some its contemporary challenges.

52. It would be necessary for UNESCO to organize in the near future an exchange and evaluation meeting for all existing networks such as the UNITWIN/UNESCO Chairs programme, UNISPAR, and the Commonwealth Secretariat. The meeting would promote the sharing of experience, reveal the factors responsible to their relative successes or failures, and co-ordinate and strengthen projects that offer the most viable solution to the problem of the Africa region.

53. The African Regional Convention and the international recommendation on the recognition of studies and diplomas should be strengthened through the promotion of academic and professional mobility of students, and academics. This would support the on-going regional integration process by using culture and education as a basis for political and economic unity. It would be desirable to strengthen associations whose aim is to *harmonise the qualification awarded by higher education institutions in Africa* (e.g. CAMES). UNESCO should take the lead in mobilising major regional and international organisations to create a region-wide mobility programme for students and academics. This has been done on other regions, one example being RIMA (Réseau International de Mobilité Académique or the International network for academic mobility) established by MERCOSUR.

54. We would further suggest that UNESCO works in concert with bilateral and multilateral co-operation agencies like the Commonwealth Secretariat and AUPELF-UREF, etc., for the early creation of *priority area networks.* These should include a research network on the use of new information and communicatins technologies, a network of teaching-learning resource units, a network of research units in education devoted to priority areas for Africa development, which could be grouped under UNESCO Chairs in

Education. UNESCO should whenever possible, mobilize resources for co-operation on areas of common concern.

55. To respect the right to cultural diversity, we would urge UNESCO to assist in the creation of a *network of lusophone institutions of higher education* and to intensify its support to the activities of association of Portuguese and Spanish speaking universities as one other means of reinforcing South-South co-operation. The development of graduate programmes in Portuguese-speaking countries should be supported. Other regional networks could contribute their expertise in this area.

56. It goes without saying that the participation of students, teachers and researchers in the meetings and networks depends on relative ease of procedures for obtaining visas. We urge UNESCO to sensitise its Members States to this particular problem, so that they can *simplify existing administrative procedures for obtaining visas.*

57. Given these challenges and the expected roles of institutions of higher education, it would be necessary *to reinforce the higher education unit of the Regional Office of UNESCO in Dakar (BREDA).* The unit should play a more active role in the envisaged regioinalisation strategies and also be the key actor in the synergy-building missions described in the above proposals. The Regional Advisory Committee on Co-operation in Education in Africa should include representatives of government organisations and NGOs working in the field of higher education.

58. It is further suggested that, as part of the NGO consultation process, UNESCO/Dakar organize a meeting with the participation of AAU, AUPELF-UREF, ACU, AULP and AIUP, as well as sub-regional organisations and bilateral co-operation and inter-governmental organisations such as CAMES, OAU, ECA, the Commonwealth Secretariat, etc., as a means of facilitating co-ordination into operative action plans as soon as possible.

59. We recommend that, with the assistance of UNESCO, stakeholders and organisations involved in the development

of higher education in the region should translate these proposals into operative action plans as soon as possible.

60. We suggest further that the report of the Regional Consultation in Dakar be tabled at the next MINEDAF and the next summit of the OAU.

61. *Finally, we request UNESCO to convene a meting of experts at the end of the year 2001, to evaluate in the implementation of the recommendations of the Regional Consultation.*

Adopted in Dakar
4th April 1997
The Regional Consultation

List of Abreviations

AAU: Association of African Universities

AUPELF-UREF: Agence francophone pour I'enseignement superiéur et la recherche

ACU: Association of Commonwealth Universities

AULP: Association of the Universities in Portuguese-speaking countries

AIUP: Association Internationale des Présidents d'Universitiés

CAMES: Conseil African et malgache pour I'enseignement supérieur

ECA: Economic Commission for Africa

5

Arab States

Beirut Declaration on Higher Education in the Arab States for the XXIst Century[1]

We, the participants to the Arab States Regional Conference on Higher Education for the XXlst Century, held in Beirut, Lebanon, from 2 to 5 March 1998,

1. Recalling the terms of the Universal Declaration of Human Rights, which states that 'higher education shall be equally accessible to all on the basis of merit' (article 26.1), and that such 'education shall be directed to the full development of the human personality and to the strengthening of respect for human rights and fundamental freedoms' (article 26.2); Ratifying the contents of the Convention on the struggle against discrimination in the field of education (1960), which states that the Signatory States commit themselves 'to..., offer all people alike higher education on the basis of a real equality and to the skills of each individual...' (article IV);
2. Recognising the importance of the analysis and recommendations of the *UNESCO Policy Paper for Change and Development in Higher Education,* the International Commission on Education for the XXlst

1. Arab Regional Conference on Higher Education, Beirut, Lebanon, 2–5 March 1998.

Century, and the World Commission on Culture and Development;

3. Pointing out the view of the International Commission on Education for the XXIst Century that education throughout life should be based on four pillars: learning to know, learning to do, learning to live together, and learning to be, and that universities have a duty to carry out research that should contribute to solving the most serious problems facing developing countries;

4. Taking into account the recommendations made in United Nations, via (a) *An agenda for peace,* that contains principles and suggestions bearing on the preventive measures that will protect peace, as well as effective actions for restoring peace when uncontainable conflicts emerge, and (b) *An agenda for development,* that sets the conceptual bases for fostering a sustainable and permanent human development. Also highlighting the need of the Region for a just and comprehensive peace allowing for learning opportunities for all and pacing the way for the attainment of development;

5. Noting that the Arab States share common historical, language and cultural traditions and heritage yet they show diversity with regard to demography, economic means, and educational traditions;

6. Pointing out that the globalisation of economies and professional services and the rapid growth and in-depth transformation of information and communication technologies have resulted in increased demands for specialised professionals in every endeavour of life capable of sustaining high standards calling for an increased appreciation of the role of higher education in the development and advancement of societies and for a revision of training and working methods of higher education graduates;

7. Acknowledging that significant progress has been made in recent years in the development and strengthening of higher education in the Arab States, leading to improved

student access and more equitable representation of different social groups among graduates;

8. Supporting the initiative taken by H.R.H Prince Talal bin Abdel-Aziz AI-Saud concerning the establishment of an Open Arab University as a model for unifying Arab efforts in the field of higher education;

9. Emphasising the recommendations of the six ALECSO conferences of Ministers responsible for Higher Education and Scientific Research in Arab States since 1981, and those of the Fifth Regional Conference of Ministers of Education and those Responsible for Economic Planning (Cairo, 1994);

10. Noting that the main issues in higher education in the Arab States encompass the following:

    (a) Higher education in the Arab States is under considerable stain, due to high rates of population growth and increasing social demand for higher education, which lead states and institutions to increase student enrolment, often without adequate allocated financial resources;

    (b) A number of Arab States are facing blockade, occupation, and external impediments and constraints limiting the expansion and development of higher education;

    (c) Although general rate of female enrolment in higher education is close to those observed at the international level, all Arab States look up to increasing this rate;

    (d) Management of higher education institutions is still heavily centralised, calling for more flexibility and for the participation in decision-making of all concerned parties;

    (e) The lack of close links between higher education institutions and general education and between universities and other post-secondary institutions, and weaknesses in students' orientation into the

various streams of higher education on the basis of their skills and interests, have contributed to inflated enrolment in some disciplines and to obvious lower enrolment in applied and technological disciplines, to low internal efficiency, and to low quality of graduates, and led to pressures on institutions to provide remedial programmes in order to improve the quality of enrolled students;

(f) Higher education institutions have, in most cases, not developed adequate programmes and projects to serve local communities and participate in their development;

(g) The development of private and open universities, and on non-university institutions, is recent in most of the Arab States, and, thus far, has not alleviated pressures on public universities in such a manner as a to permit the development, the diversification, and the expansion of higher education;

(h) Status and conditions of higher education teaching personnel, while enormously varied among Arab Sates, do not often match some of the international standards as set in the Recommendation concerning the Status and Conditions of Higher Education Teaching Personnel adopted in 1997 by UNESCO General Conference;

(i) Higher education institutions should be more sensitive to students' concerns, taking into account their needs in all endeavours of life during years of study, as to selection, curricula, teaching, and transition to working life. These institutions should allow students and their representatives to actively participate in decision-making concerning their academic and social life within the institution;

(j) There is a need to promote new teaching and learning processes that better serve the development of scientific thinking skills;

(k) As a result of international developments in science and technology, new demands have emerged for

teaching personnel and researchers to increase co-operation with industry, and for continuing education of graduates;

(l) Lack of highly qualified graduates in some disciplines is often accompanied with unemployment and under-employment of great numbers of graduates in other disciplines, while significant numbers of highly qualified Arab scholars lead academic careers abroad with little impact on higher education and scientific research in the Arab States.

In view of the above, we do hereby declare the following:

1. Higher education is essential for any country to achieve sustainable and global development. It is also essential for the enhancement of citizens' participation in public life, for social mobility, and for the achievement of harmony, justice, and just and comprehensive peace, at both internal and internationa levels, on the basis of the respect for human rights, active participation of citizens, and mutual respect.

2. Higher education should aim at the following: (a) to educate well-aware, autonomous and responsible citizens committed to national and universal principles, capable of dealing with the challenges of the Country and of lifelong learning, (b) to provide highly trained professionals to meet the needs of government, the professions, and the productive and service sectors, (c) to provide expertise to assist in economic and social development, and in scientific and technological research, (d) to help conserve and disseminate national and regional cultures, drawing on the contributions from each generation, (e) to provide critical and detached perspectives concerning the strategic options and to contribute to human renewal by active contribution to the production of scientific knowledge, taking into account ethical issues, and addressing planetary challenges (such as population growth, peace, environment, etc.), (f) to undertake research and scholarship which contribute to

the understanding, the anticipation and the solving of the most serious problems of the Region.

3. Determined efforts are necessary to further increase access to higher education to all groups of society. Open learning systems and other systems of education relying on modern technology can play a major role in widening access and can contribute to higher cultural achievements of Arab States citizens, if they are provided with the means to ensure quality. Diversification of institutions and programmes can also play a significant role on alleviating the strains put on traditional institutions by the ever growing social demand for higher education due to rapid growth rate of population and appeal of higher education for large sectors of society.

4. Arab States should devote determined efforts to improve general education as to ensure that graduates of this level of education master the essential competencies needed for life, including those necessary for the pursuit of higher education endeavours. Higher education institutions should actively participate in the efforts leading to improvement of pre-university education.

5. Arab States and their higher education institutions should adopt specific national and institutional plans of action in order to increase the participation in higher education of disadvantaged groups at all levels and in all disciplines, particularly females and the citizens under strenuous conditions due to occupation or blockade. They should work in co-operation with regional and international agencies in order to provide learning opportunities to deprived students and to permit them enrolment in higher education institutions within their countries.

6. All higher education systems and institutions should give a high priority to ensuring the quality of programmes, teaching, and outcomes. Structures, procedures, and standards for quality assurance should be developed at the regional and national levels commensurate with international guidelines while providing for variety

according to the specificities of each country, institution, or programme. Further, higher education institutions need appropriate financial and human resources to achieve higher quality of education.

7. Modern information and communications technology (ICT) is already making radical changes in methods of teaching and learning in higher education by both on-campus and distance education students. It has the potential to make positive impact on quality, relevance, access and cost of higher education, if direct access to technical and cultural information resources is provided, and rapid communication among teachers and researchers is facilitated. These technologies allow for the establishment of networks between institutions and scholars and enhance their development and efficiency. They also contribute in the provision of courses and degree-awarding programmes through multiple and advanced means, thus breaking through the traditional barriers of space and time. The virtual capacity of these developments in teaching tools is almost limitless for improving distance, open and life-long learning, if the adequate conditions are ensured.

8. Access to scientific knowledge is an essential element of cultural and intellectual understanding and the further development of higher education institutions. With the increased emergence of digitalisation and the increasing reliance on communication technologies as a means of storage and transfer of scholarly information, open and affordable access to communication networks becomes an important and indispensable element of quality of higher education institutions and programmes. Governments of Arab States should ensure that informatic and communication network infrastructure, personal computer facilities, and human resources training, now a globally recognised prerequisite for the normal functioning of higher education institutions and research centres, are adequately provided. Regional and international co-operation and development organisations are called upon to allocate technical and financial resources to support these developments in the Arab States.

9. While recognising that globalisation is a trend that could not be ignored nor avoided, it should not lead to dominance of some cultures and value systems on some others, nor to the emergence of new forms of hegemony. To this effect, it is of vital importance that every effort should be made to protect and promote the strengths of the Arab and Islamic culture and civilisation as part of the major intellectual cultures in the world; at the same time, dialogue and cultural exchanges between the Arab States and the other world states should be maintained.

10. The concept of lifelong learning is of utmost importance. In rapidly changing economies, the labour market will constantly require new and various skills. Hence, mechanisms must be developed at higher education level to allow workforce in all fields to upgrade their skills and develop new competencies at regular intervals throughout their lives. Higher education institutions must offer learning opportunities in response to diverse and new demands and work co-operatively with other agencies and employers to ensure that appropriate and flexible programmes and courses are widely available and accessible to all citizens who need to update their knowledge and skills in order to effectively deal with such matters as population, labour, environment, etc. At the same time, higher education must take a leading role in the evolution of the world of work to better meet sustainable development requirements.

11. The involvement of all key stakeholders in decision-making in higher education institutions is of utmost importance, particularly the academics, the students, and the productive and service sectors, alongside with representatives of governmental agencies. Experience has demonstrate the value of such participation in enlightening the visions necessary for decision-making and the formulation of balanced higher education policy, both system wide and institutionally.

12. In view of its multiplier effects on social, cultural and economic development, public funding of higher education

should be considered as a investment, the return of it being as much important as investment in all sectors. However, better use of allocated resources and other funding sources must be sought after as well as developing partnerships with the private sector and the society.

13. Co-operation among the Arab States, especially in higher education, through academic exchanges, twinning and networking arrangements, can make significant contributions in addressing major higher education policy matters, and facilitating the sharing of pioneering expertise and experiences. Arab co-operation is made easier in view of the common linguistic and cultural heritage of the Arab States. This co-operation should be reinforced especially at graduate studies, scientific research programmes, institutional research and development.

14. Freedom of movement of students and access to academic institutions across Arab States frontiers will strengthen the Arab cultural development and contribute efficiently to Arab integration in higher education.

15. There is a pressing need to develop a plan of action and guidelines to further develop higher education in the Arab States, especially related to the key issues of relevance, quality, management and finance, and co-operation which are defined as follows:

    RELEVANCE refers to the fit between what higher education institutions provide and what society expects from them. Relevance requires from higher education to make an enhanced contribution to the development of the society as a whole, encompassing the development of the education system. Relevance also requires reciprocal harmonisation with the world of work and the requirements of sustainable global development. Relevance requires higher education to contribute to the preservation, the enlargement, the deepening, and the dissemination of knowledge in such a manner as to help humankind solve the problems it faces. It also requires safeguarding cultural diversity, the quest for just and global peace and respect of human rights.

QUALITY refers to standards of inputs, processes, and outputs of a system, an institution, or a programme. It has no meaning without relevance. Quality is a multi-dimensional concept and embraces all the functions and activities of higher education, i.e. academic programmes, research, and community services, in all their features and components: infrastructure, equipment, human resources, students, objectives, nature and content of programmes, delivery modes and implementation practices, academic and socio-cultural environment, etc. Quality mechanisms are implemented through continuous assessments and comparisons between observed and intended process and constant search for the sources of dysfunctions to correct them.

MANAGEMENT AND FINANCE cover, on one hand, issues related to internal management of institutions, funding and resources, and, on the other hand, the relations of higher education institutions with the state, and other stakeholders. Higher education authorities and institutions need to adopt long-term strategies aiming at embodying the institutions in the whole social tissue they serve, i.e. the Governmental bodies, the professions, the education sector, the productive and service sectors, and the socio-cultural environment. As for financing, despite the general trend towards diversifying sources of funding, governmental support for higher education and research remains essential to ensure achievement of educational and social missions of educational institutions. Furthermore, with the extension of private investment in higher education, appropriate mechanisms of accreditation and monitoring should be developed to guarantee access, equity, quality, and the rights of students.

CO-OPERATION at the national, regional, and international levels through advanced methods and mechanisms fit for the XXIst Century is essential for higher education institutions in order for them to adequately fulfil the missions entrusted with them.

PLAN OF ACTION

Based on the principles, observations, and recommendations set out in the Declaration on Higher Education in the Arab Stats for the XXIst Century adopted by the Conference, and considering the need for the renewal of systems through the adoption of new policies and paradigms for higher education founded on such concepts as globalisation of knowledge, lifelong learning, sustainable development, preservation of cultural diversity, transparency and accountability, and involvement of all stakeholders, the following recommendations were adopted by the Conference:

First: **The Arab States** must fulfil their commitments to higher education and meet the pledges made at regional and international conferences with regard to the provision of adequate structures and human and financial resources as to enable higher education to adequately face the challenges of the XXIst Century. This includes the following:

(a) setting up of policies and legislations as well as establishment of effective mechanisms dealing with the overall governance of higher education system and institutions, with due consideration to the promotion of institutional autonomy and the participation of all sectors concerned;

(b) establishment of rules and regulations to ensure the protection, at higher education institutions, of basic rights (e.g., access by merit, equality of treatment, etc.) and freedoms, especially academic freedom;

(c) establishment of accountability measures proper to achieve stated goals, and to ensure quality of inputs, processes and outcomes;

(d) enabling higher education institutions fulfil their multiple duties towards society;

(e) providing for modern communication technology in order to ensure unconditional access to accumulated human knowledge;

(f) promoting partnerships with industry, and productive and service sectors, and other governmental or non-governmental relevant institutions.

Second: **Higher Education Institutions** must define their missions in harmony with the overall aims and principles as defined by the Declaration and Plan of action approved by the Conference. These missions should be translated into well-defined objectives, with allocation of the required resources, and the establishment of concrete mechanisms proper to ensure adequate monitoring and evaluation of progress and achievements based on observable indicators. A framework for evaluation and monitoring should thus be established and strengthened in all institutions, with proper structures and resources.

Third: **Joint Action Plans** must be established to ensure the further development of higher education in the Arab countries, optimize efficiency, and prevent duplication of efforts. Co-operation between organisations which promote the development of human resources, particularly within the framework of institutionalised networks, at the global, regional, and national levels, offers great potentials for the enhanced mobilisation of resources. Responsibility for this mobilization lies on international and regional organizations dealing with inter-university co-operation, as well as the associations of universities and higher education institutions, private and public universities, institutions of research, development organizations and agencies, governmental and non-governmental institutions. Concerned agencies active in the Arab Region, particularly ALECSO, ISESCO, ABEGS, the Association of Arab Universities, the Arab Federation of Councils for Scientific Research, and the Arab Federation for Technical Education, could play an important role in strengthening existing networks and in building new regional networks leading to the solution of pressing problems of higher education and of the societies of the Arab States. The

Association of Islamic Universities, and other cross-regional and international organizations could also play a role in finding solutions to problems of common interests. Partnerships with world organizations and institutions are particularly sought after. The mass media should also be called on to support these initiatives.

Fourth: **UNESCO,** through the joint efforts of Headquarters, Regional Offices, and its centres, institutes or units specialized in higher education in other regions, in co-operation with other UN agencies such as UNDP and the Economic and Social Commission for Western Asia (ESCWA), Higher Education NGOs, and UNESCO Chairs and Networks, must reinforce its programmes of higher education in the Arab States, including its contribution to the development of the whole education system. In particular, UNESCO must reinforce its unit in Higher Education at its Beirut Office, so that this may, in conjunction with the other relevant bodies and units:

(a) encourage studies, projects and research activities to support the elaboration of public policies and other initiatives related to higher education, and promote public understanding of the value of higher education. In particular, UNESCO should sponsor regional projects aiming at (1) the development and implementation of new ideas concerning the governance of higher education systems and institutions, (2) the development and sustainable implementation of a framework for quality assurance, (3) the implementation of structures dealing with research and institutional development, (4) the elaboration of common understandings as regards to the role, functions and functioning of higher education private institutions, and (5) the elaboration of programmes aiming at establishing close links between social problems and concerns and higher education institutions and support for their implementation;

(b) provide managers of higher education with opportunities for the discussion of issues, current problems, and long-term challenges related to higher education;

(c) foster training for teaching personnel and managers of higher education institutions;

(d) co-ordinate the implementation of UNESCO/UNITWIN Chairs Programme in the Arab States and, in particular, stimulate the development of centres of excellence, through the creation of specialized networks, with special attention given to networks for distance education, teachers training, the utilization of information and communication technologies, and institutional development in higher education;

(e) work in partnership with regional and international organizations, associations, and networks.

In addition, UNESCO is called upon to reinforce its current programmes, carried out by the UNESCO Cairo Office, for assisting Arab universities in developing their co-operation infrastructure and acquiring the knowledge and skills of information and communication technologies and in using these technologies for upgrading the quality of their teaching in fundamental and applied sciences.

Member States and donor organizations of the Arab Region are called upon to support UNESCO to enable it carry on the above mentioned programmes and activities for the benefit of all Arab States.

Fifth: The elaboration of decisions and plans taken by all the bodies mentioned above should be based on the principles stated below.

1. Relevance

(i) Access to higher education

1. Arab governments must expand and diversify opportunities for every citizen to upgrade his or her qualifications and

develop higher-level personal, academic and citizenship competencies such as those provided in higher education institutions. Appropriate strategies should elaborated and implemented and serious efforts should be made to increase participation rates in higher education, particularly for those already involved in the world of work or dropouts of the educational system, through flexible programmes and schedules, allowing for part-time study and diversified short qualifying or diploma-driven programmes.

2. Distance education and open learning constitute important alternative delivery systems of higher education. Governments should provide the legislative and regulatory frameworks in order for such schemes to be developed. They also should encourage such initiatives and facilitate their operation through easy access to modern communication networks and recognition of the qualifications earned without neglecting the basic requirements for quality assurance and the relevance of outcomes.

(ii) The world of work

3. In order to facilitate the elaboration of national educational plans and to improve the capacity of higher education institutions to align their policies with national priorities, governments should create or reinforce planning mechanisms to monitor trends and needs of the labour market, in close, continuous, and interactive partnership with higher education institutions and the productive and service sectors. "Observatories" may be created to monitor short- and long-term trends of the world of work and the harmonization needed between these trends and higher education policies and programmes.

4. Higher education institutions must help shape the labour market by identifying the needs of the social and economic sectors for new professionals and specialists. New disciplines and specializations should be introduced into the curriculum of higher education institutions. At the same time, job opportunities should be created for the graduates of these disciplines by a joint effort of

governments, enterprises, and the higher education community. Higher education institutions should also provide school dropouts and those already in the workforce flexible opportunities to upgrade their competencies and knowledge levels, as well as to profit from retraining and career-switching.

5. Special attention should be given to the development of study programmes at the professional level, particularly by introducing or expanding higher colleges of technology, and at the graduate level, by expanding master's and Ph.D. programmes, with due regard to designing specializes learning material of specific disciplines of high quality relevant to societal needs and delivered through new information and communication technologies.

6. Curricula should be organized to stimulate the entrepreneurial skills of students, grounded on flexible, innovative, and interdisciplinary approaches, as to break the general trend towards the dependence of most graduates on public employment. Incubator projects which help create new enterprises should be fostered with the support of governments, the productive and service sectors, and local communities. In addition, more industry-based projects and new paradigms of university-industry partnership must be instituted. UNESCO, UNIDO, UNDP, the World Bank, AGFUND, Islamic Development Bank, and other development funding agencies could be sought after to assist in this matter.

(iii) Responsibility towards other education levels

7. Higher education must take up its duties towards other levels of education. This is needed not only to ensure that students are better prepared for higher education, but also to ensure that pupils experience less failures, stay longer in schools, and are given educational and guidance services appropriate to their abilities and interests. To this effect, auxiliary educational services should be created at all levels of education and services should be provided to all students who require them. Moreover, in view of the ever increasing rates of illiteracy in some Arab States, of

the negative effects of illiteracy on economic and social development, and of the enormous human potential of the hundred thousands of students enrolled in higher education, higher education community should take a leading role in combating illiteracy, particularly among girls and women.

8. To act on its responsibility and role towards the whole education system, higher education in the Arab States should actively participate (a) in the improvement of the quality of general education, (b) in the renovation of teacher and other educational personnel training schemes aiming at more professionalization, (c) in conducting research on social and educational variables that may reduce school failure and dropout, and in recommending appropriate educational approacnes and policy alternatives, etc., (d) in the development, in close, continuous, and interactive partnership with education authorities and institutions, of activity programmes and direct services to the education community aiming at helping the education system each the objectives of education for all as set in Jomtien Conference (1990). Networks and Chairs in educational sciences should be created and reinforced as part of the strategy to achieve these ends.

(iv) Major social problems

9. Higher education institutions should contribute to the development of students' personal awareness, commitment, and capacity to cope, at the personal as well as at the professional levels, with the major social issues facing humankind, such as population, poverty, illiteracy, public health, protection of the environment, protection of cultural diversity, social participation, human rights and international understanding, etc. All higher education study programmes should include courses dealing with these issues with appropriate concrete applications according to students' fields of specializations.

10. Arab higher education should take active par+ in facilitating access to and harnessing of modern technology and scientific

discoveries by all members of the educational community and by the public at large. It has a special responsibility, alongside with the media, towards the passage of Arab societies to information and communication age. In particular, all higher education teaching, technical, and administrative personnel, and all students of all disciplines must be provided with the necessary training that enables them to integrate new information and communication technologies into their work.

(v) Regional integration

11. Higher education institutions must promote processes aiming at Arab integration, starting at the cultural and educational levels, with the view to attain economic and political integration. The adoption of common standards for quality assessment and recognition of educational and professional qualifications constitutes a step forward toward such an integration, as well as the adoption of common core study programmes in the various professional fields. The implementation of common research projects may constitute another way towards this end. Intensive efforts should be devoted to studying the economic, social, cultural, ecological and political obstacles to integration and the strategies and actions needed to overcome these obstacles.

2. Quality

12. Each Arab State should establish a mechanism for evaluating the quality of its higher education at the systemic, institutional, programme, personnel and outcomes levels. Quality assurance methods may include academic accreditation, institutional evaluations or sector reviews by disciplines and professional areas, performance funding, competency-based approaches to professional education and training.

13. Appropriate emphasis needs to be placed on the renewal of curricula, on continuous assessment of teaching and learning approaches and the adoption of new ones, as well as the promotion of multidisciplinary studies. The

utilization of multi-media and the Internet must all be used, with due consideration to promote interaction between students, teachers, and managers.

14. Governments and institutions of higher education must adopt appropriate strategies for the recruitment and training of teaching personnel, for their further professional development and for recognition of their achievements. Legislative bodies, governments, and higher education institutions should take the necessary measures to implement the Recommendation concerning the Status and Conditions of Higher Education Teaching Personnel, approved by the 29th Session of UNESCO General Conference (Paris, 1997).

15. Each higher education institution should establish a centre for the professional development and the improvement of the teaching performance of its teaching personnel.

16. Higher education institutions should modernize libraries and take the necessary measures to provide for scientific equipment and guarantee its modernization within the framework of their long-term plans. In this context, regional and international co-operation should particularly be enhanced as to ensure to students and academics from Arab States adequate access to scientific equipment and information that could not be made available due to limited budgets and resources.

17. Higher education institutions must provide each student with orientation and study skills training, and pave the way for him to play an efficient role in society.

18. Appropriate strategies should be developed in order to strengthen research capacity at higher education institutions, including research aiming at the acquisition, the broadening, and the deepening of knowledge and publishing its results. Conducting such research should be an obligation to all members of the teaching personnel at higher education institutions. States and institutions should provide for proper structures, equipment, and staff, as well as the necessary financial support as to ensure

the involvement of teaching personnel in research and publication activities. Co-operate programmes at the national, regional, and international levels should be encouraged, including linking of higher education institutions, centres, and laboratories to government and industry research laboratories.

3. Management and Financial Resources

(i) Governance and management systems

19. Autonomy of higher education institutions of the Arab States should be fostered. This includes, among other things, the freedom to select staff and students, to determine the conditions under which they remain in the institution, to determine the curriculum and degree standards, to allocate resources for different activities, and to select research topics. Institutional autonomy should be accompanied by a high level of responsibility and accountability and the widest possible participation of students, faculty, and administration in decision-making.

20. Governments should consider creating or reinforcing agencies that act as buffer between concerned ministries and higher education institutions and provide advice on such matters as organization, accountability and quality assurance, allocation of resources, and the administration of grants and financial assistance, with due consideration to the fact that higher education implies that its appraisal cannot be restricted to economic quantitative indicators alone.

21. Opportunities should be given, wherever possible, to government, and the professional and productive sectors to participate in decision-making concerning management and organization of higher education.

22. Management capacities in higher education should be strengthened by appropriate training and staff development programmes for all managers, especially those in executive positions, the adoption of clear job descriptions and decision-making channels, the

improvement of managerial procedures, and the introduction of computerized management systems.

23. Each higher education institution should establish a unit staffed with experienced qualified personnel with the mandate to conduct the necessary studies and research and to propose strategies and actions aiming at the institutional development and the improvement of management. Its studies can include, inter alia, such matters as planning and management, evaluation of training and service programmes and the introduction of new ones, the development of distance education schemes, the condition of women and the strategies to enhance their participation at the different levels of the institution. To this end, UNESCO Chairs and Networks could be developed and implemented in the Arab States.

(ii) Financial resources

24. Arab States must renew the commitments made by them at the Social Development Summit in Copenhagen and at other world bodies to "make new and additional resources available" and thus increase their budgets allocated to education in general and to higher education in particular, measured as a percentage of their gross national product.

25. Even though the state should remain the main party responsible for funding higher education, diversification of funding sources, in particular, through cost recovery of extra-academic activities, and encouragement of various income-generating activities, such as contract research, cultural and academic services, short-term courses, etc... should actively be sought after. This could only be achieved by the involvement of all stakeholders, the public and private sectors, local communities, academic associations, and non-governmental organizations. Legislative bodies should play a leading role in the matter by the adoption of appropriate measures to encourage diversification of funding sources with due consideration to ensuring access to higher education according to merit, and equity.

26. In order to assure high-quality research, it is required to adopt adequate systems for public and private support to research undertaken at higher education institutions, as well as to double the existing level of funding.
27. The complementary role of private institutions of higher education must be recognized. Governments should provide a legal framework to regulate private higher education institutions and develop appropriate mechanisms for accredition, diploma recognition, and licensing, it addition to setting standards for quality assurance and adequacy of the required educational facilities and services.

4. Co-operation

28. Each institution of higher education must envisage the creation of a specialized unit for managing Arab and international co-operation. These units must develop international linkages, such as those for the exchange of students and teaching personnel, and other academic co-operation activities. As well, they must co-operate within the framework of the activities of international organizations and bilateral agreements.
29. International and Regional organizations must support projects aiming at reinforcing co-operation between higher education institutions through the establishment and strengthening of higher education networks, and support to the activities of existing associations, especially the Association of Arab Universities, the Arab Federation of Councils for Scientific Research and the Arab Federation for Technical Education.
30. Higher education institutions should strengthen their endogenous and co-operative capacities related to priority issues in the Arab States. Centres of excellence can have a positive impact on the solution of major social problems related to the environment, demographic growth, sustainable development, research on higher education, educational research, institutional management, teaching staff professional development, arabization of higher

education, provision of communication technologies, technology transfer, the protection of cultural heritage, etc....

31. The exchange of knowledge and experience between higher education institutions in the Arab States must be carried out in a spirit of solidarity and be the basis for co-operation agreements between them. Within their capacity, UNESCO and other international and regional governmental and non-governmental organizations should respond to the request to provide technical assistance to smaller and poor countries.

32. A special effort must be undertaken to re-build the higher education system in Palestine and in occupied territories, to remove the barriers which the military occupation places that prevent the free movement of students and faculty members, and that hinder access to research and study. Concerned parties should endeavour to stop all measures that threaten the safety and security of students and staff of institutions of higher education. At the same time, appropriate pressures must be exerted to remove obstacles to the free exchange of students and academics between Palestine and the Arab States. Finally, Arab institutions of Higher education are urged to continue their policies supporting access of qualified Palestinian students to higher education.

33. The establishment of the Arab Open University must be encouraged in the light of the results of the studies pertaining to it.

34. Regional co-operation projects in the field of teaching staff personnel and their professional development should be reinforced. Arab States are urged to encourage the establishment of the Arab University for Graduate Studies and Scientific Research.

35. A series of actions should be undertaken by governments and higher education systems in the Arab States following the recommendations of the Regional Committee

responsible for the application of the Convention on the Recognition of Studies, Diplomas and Degree of Higher Education in the Arab States; in particular:

- exchange of information and documentation with regional committees of other regions;
- development of inter-regional co-operation among national documentation centres for the recognition of studies and diplomas;
- development of capacities in view of collection, treatment and dissemination of information in order to facilitate the recognition of studies and diplomas in higher education;
- development of research aiming at facilitating the recognition of studies and diplomas, on subjects or themes such as academic and professional mobility, recognition of skills and experiences, etc...

36. Within the framework of the Convention on the-Recognition of Studies, Diplomas and Degrees of Higher Education, governments, institutions of higher education, professional bodies and international organizations must encourage student, academic and professional mobility to benefit the process of economic, educational, political and cultural integration in the Arab States and to develop mutually accepted standards for the recognition of diplomas. In this action, attention should be paid to incorporate the Arabic dimension as an integral part of teaching and research. Furthermore, all efforts should be made to remove practical, administrative and legal obstacles to academic exchange at institutional, national and international levels.

5. Final Recommendations

37. Governments, higher education institutions, and all stakeholders concerned with the development of higher education in the Arab States must translate the recommendations of this plan of action into operational projects as soon as possible.

38. For improving the systems of co-operation in the Arab States, an evaluation of existing networks, including those established within the framework of UNITWIN/UNESCO Charis programme, should be carried out.
39. UNESCO, with the support of governments and other organizations, must convene a meeting of experts in 2002 of 2003 to evaluate and follow-up the implementation of the recommendations of Beirut Conference.

6

Asia and the Pacific

Declaration about higher education in Asia and the Pacific

We, participants of the Asia and Pacific Regional Conference on Higher Education National Strategies and Regional Co-operation for the 21st Century,[1]

1. **Recalling,** on one hand, the terms of the Universal Declaration of Human Rights, which states in article 26 that "every person has the right to education"...and that "higher education shall be accessible to all, on the basis of merit", and, on the other hand, the UNESCO Constitution which encourages institutional exchanges in the area of education;
2. **Recognizing** the importance of the analysis and recommendations of the Policy Paper on Change and Development in Higher Education launched by UNESCO in 1995 and resulting from a world-wide reflection on the role of higher education in society; the view of the International Commission on Education for the XXI Century that "Universities in developing countries have a duty to carry out research that should contribute to solving the most serious problems facing these countries"; and the conclusion of the World Commission on Culture

1. Tokyo, Japan, 8-10 July 1997.

and Development that development is "a far more complex undertaking than had been originally thought" and that it should not be "seen as a single, uniform linear path for this would inevitably eliminate cultural diversity and experimentation, and dangerously limit humankind's creative capacities in the face of a treasured past and an unpredictable future";

3. **Noting** the exceptional diversity of and variety within the Asia and Pacific region with regard to demography, religion, culture, ethnicity and education, with the most populous nations existing alongside small states, and the region including not only some of the fasted growing and wealthiest economies but also some of the poorest; and further noting that this region has been characterized as the cradle of civilization, of the world's great religions and philosophies, and the earliest educational systems;

4. **Pointing out** that the rapid growth and in-depth transformation of societies and of key regional economies has resulted in a new appreciation of the role of higher education in technological development and increased demands for specialized professionals, while the increasing use of new information and communications technologies provides exciting possibilities for innovation in course design and delivery, for access to intellectual resources and for building new networks of experts and institutions, thus requiring that the concept and practices of lifelong learning be further developed;

5. **Acknowledging** that as the countries of the region draw closer together through trade, improved transportation and rapid communications into a seemingly common destiny, each one is consciously fostering its own sense of identity and nationhood, and rediscovering its cultural heritage and the value of its languages. In recent years, the region has demonstrated impressive capacity for innovation, especially in the application of science and technology, and exceptionally high rates of economic growth. In 1960, Asia had only 4 per cent of the world-wide GNP, whereas it now accounts for 25 per cent, with

this figure being predicted to reach 30 per cent by the year 2000. However, in many professional fields there are on-going serious shortages in the supply of qualified professionals while rapid growth has resulted in major urban and social problems, and serious degradation of the environment;

6. **Observing** that significant progress has been made in recent years in the development and strengthening of higher education within the countries of the region, particularly leading to improved student access, strengthened research and postgraduate programmes, more equitable representation of different social groups among graduates, renewed curricula and adoption of new teaching and delivery methods, and enhanced institutional management and strategic planning capacity. At the same time, many nations of the region are still far from achieving a desirable number and quality of graduates required by the new economic situation;

7. **Nothing** that the main trends in higher education in the region include the following:

   - Higher education across the region is under considerable strain. Student enrolments continue to increase resulting in further pressure on public funding for higher education institutions; the level of financial resources is often considered inadequate are there is widespread evidence of experimentation to diversify funding sources, including reinforced links with the productive sector;

   - Gender inequality, particularly among students, academic staff and senior management, continues to be an issue of considerable concern at all levels in the majority of countries. In a number of countries at the undergraduate level, female participation has approached or exceeded 50 per cent of enrolments, but generally female students are concentrated in "traditional" feminine disciplines. In many countries, women constitute no more than 20 per cent or 30 per cent of academics, while in other instances women are practically excluded from participation in higher education at all;

- In many countries, higher education institutions are heavily concentrated in urban areas, whereas the majority of the population lives in rural areas, thus requiring new mechanisms to address rural disadvantage; other disadvantaged sectors of society, such as those with disabilities, are not adequately served;
- As a result of international developments in science and technology and their impact on both economic development and social lifestyle, new demands have emerged for researchers, technicians and other specialised professionals and for an increased level of co-operation with industry in R&D. Frequently there are serious mismatches in the demand for and supply of highly trained personnel, especially in countries undergoing rapid economic growth and industrialization;
- Dramatic increases have occurred in the number of private higher education institutions, with accompanying diversification in structures, curriculum and teaching methods and management approaches resulting from both internal factors (such as changes in academic disciplines and new instructional methods) and external factors (such as population growth, the need to cater for more diverse clienteles and changing labour market requirements). Particularly important has been the development of non-university institutions and the establishment of open universities and distance learning systems;
- There is increasing concern in many countries with regard to the quality of courses, facilities, staff and graduates and the deterioration of infrastructure (laboratories, buildings and libraries) and a lack of scientific equipment;
- Unemployment of graduates especially in countries undergoing rapid transition, and lack of highly

qualified professionals from less developed nations, have unfortunate long-term consequences for a number of countries of the region;

- Many leaders of higher education in the region see the need for better integration of western concepts and values with Eastern philosophy and culture;
- In many countries, teaching and learning procedures are often based largely on memorization and recall, which do not develop analytical and problem-solving skills. Frequently, undue emphasis is placed on the immediate utility of knowledge rather than on fundamental wisdom while the persistence of dogmatic approaches in education seriously hinders the development of enquiring minds;
- The lack of close links, in many countries, between universities and other post—secondary institutions, and between higher education institutions and secondary school is a matter of on-going concern.

8. **Recognizing** the various initiative taken over the past decade by several governmental and non-governmental organizations and higher education institutions *(e.g. debates in the framework of APEC for the formulation of a regional programme in higher education for human resource development; restoration of the activities of the SEAMEO Regional Institute for Higher Education and Development (RIHED); the recent formation of the Association of Universities of Asia and Pacific (AUAP); establishment of the UMAP University Mobility in Asia and the Pacific Programme (UMAP) which aims at promoting student mobility at undergraduate level; the formation of the UNESCO-supported Asia Pacific Higher Education Network (APHEN) to foster research collaboration; progress with the UNESCO Chairs, UNITWIN and UNISPAR Programmes and the conclusions of various conferences on higher education issues and reforms hosted by different countries of the region;*
9. **Taking into account** the conclusions of the *Sixth Regional Conference of Ministers of Education and those Responsible*

for Economic Planing in Asia and the Pacific, organized by UNESCO in co-operation with ESCAP, which called for support for regional and national programmes to encourage mobility, networking and quality monitoring in higher education; Resolution No. 1.6 adopted by the twenty-eighth session of the General Conference of UNESCO in November 1995, which called for the strengthening of regional co-operation in higher education in Asia and the Pacific notably by taking appropriate measures to establish a Regional Programme in Higher Education in UNESCO's Bangkok Office and which invited the Director General to ensure that development of the programme be discussed "in a regional conference on higher education for the preparation of a world conference on higher education planned for 1998"; and the results of various recent major meetings within the region, including those at Armidale, Penang, Tokyo and Xiamen, and the instructional Conference which took place in Manila where a special Declaration was approved.

We, the participants of the Asia and Pacific Regional Conference on National Strategies and Regional Co-operation for the 21st Century, assembled in Tokyo, Japan, from 8 to 10 July 1997, do hereby declare that:

1. Higher education is essential for any country to reach the necessary level of economic and social development and social mobility in order to achieve increased living standards and internal and international harmony and peace based on democracy, tolerance and mutual respect. At the end of the century, we reaffirm that the aims of higher education can be summarised as follows: to educate responsible and committed citizens, to provide highly trained professionals to meet the needs of industry, government and the professions; to provide expertise to assist in economic and social development, and in scientific and technological research; to help conserve and disseminate national and regional cultures, drawing on the contributions from each generation; to help protect values by addressing moral and ethical issues; and to provide critical and detached perspectives to assist in the

discussion of strategic options and to contribute to humanistic renewal;

2. All higher education systems and institutions should give a high priority to ensuring the quality of provision and outcomes. However, great care should be taken in making comparisons between the achievement of different higher education systems and institutions since it is not possible to arrive at one set of standards applicable to all countries and institutions and against which institutions can be assessed. Further, higher education institutions need appropriate financial and human resource to achieve quality of provision;
3. Modern information and communications technology provides considerable promise to enhance teaching learning in higher education by both on-campus and distance education students, and disabled students who tend to be denied access to traditional institutions, provide access to technical and scholarly information resources, and to facilitate communications among researchers and teachers and the establishment and enhancement of networks of institutions and scholars. Already the notion of the virtual university is being actively explored within the region. At the same time, harnessing this technology will require considerable investment in hardware, software and staff development, while deliberate efforts to ensure that the human and social interaction elements of education are not undervalued;
4. Access to scholarly communication is an essential element of cultural understanding and the further development of higher education institutions. With the increased emergence of digitalization and the increasing reliance on telecommunications as a means of scholarly communication, it is important that access to communication be open and affordable. Governments of the region should work to ensure that control of telecommunications links and software infrastructure is widely shared;
5. While recognizing that globalization and internationalization are irreversible trends, support for

these concepts should not lead to dominance or new forms of imperialism by major cultures and value systems from outside the region; rather, it is of vital importance that every effort should be taken to protect and promote the strengths of local cultures and intellectual and scholarly traditions;

6. Regional co-operation among the countries of the region, especially in higher education, can make significant contributions in addressing major policy problems, strengthening national capacity in economic and social development, and facilitating sharing of important expertise and experience. Regional co-operation is especially desirable in view of the diversity of the region and the potential for dynamic collaboration. In addition, higher education institutions should explore opportunities to promote processes aiming at regional integration without losing diversity;
7. Involvement in decision-making by all key stakeholders of higher education institutions is of utmost importance. Experience has demonstrated the value of such participation in bringing to decision-making a variety of different perspectives;
8. The concept of lifelong learning is of utmost importance. In rapidly changing economies, the labour market will constantly require new and different skills and so mechanisms must be enhanced to allow professionals to upgrade their skills at regular intervals and develop new competencies. People's needs of lifelong learning have expanded in all countries of the region. Higher education institutions thus must offer learning opportunities in response to diverse demands and work co-operatively with other agencies and employers to ensure that appropriate courses are widely available. Ready access and flexibility in timing are of utmost importance;
9. Determined efforts are necessary to increase access to higher education, especially for groups currently poorly represented. Distance education and open learning can play a major role in widening access;

10. There is an urgent need to develop a plan of action and accompanying guidelines for co-operation especially related to the key issues of relevance, quality, management and finance, and co-operation which are summarised as follows:

    Relevance refers to the fit between what higher education institutions do and what society expects of them. Relevance requires higher education to make an enhanced contribution to the development of the whole education system, notably through improved teacher education and educational research, and through reinforcement of its community service functions, including activities to eliminate poverty, hunger and disease. Relevance requires better articulation with the world of work and democratization of access to higher education, wider opportunities for participation during the various stages of life as well as the full involvement of the higher education community in the search for solutions to pressing human problems, such as population control, environmental degradation, and the quest for peace, international understanding, democracy and human rights. Academic freedom and responsible institutional autonomy particularly in the core academic functions are crucial for the achievement of the goal of relevance.

    Quality refers to standards of resourcing and provision, and the achievements or outputs of an institution or system. Quality is a multi-dimensional concept and it is not possible to arrive at one set of quality standards applicable to all countries and against which institutions can be assessed. Quality embraces all the main functions and activities of higher education: teaching and academic programmes, research and scholarship, staffing, students, infrastructure and the academic environment. It can be implemented through comparisons between observed and intended outcomes and constant analysis of the sources of dysfunction. Both internal self evaluation and external review are vital components of any well developed quality assurance system The concept of accountability is closely allied with quality. No system of higher education can fulfil its mission unless it demands the highest quality of itself. Continuous and permanent assessment is necessary to reach this objective. At the same time, it must be acknowledged that great care must be exercised in making quality assessments since it involves matters of judgement, academic values and cultural understanding.

Management and Finance covers both internal institutional management, funding and resource issues, as well as relations of higher education institutions with the state and national planning and co-ordination. Higher education institutions need to adopt forward-looking management practices which respond to the needs of their environments and which are articulated in their missions. Today, despite the general trend towards diversified sources of funding, public support for higher education and research remains essential to ensure achievement of educational and social missions. Both institutions and national agencies can develop appropriate strategies to strengthen management, planning and policy analysis capacities.

Co-operation at the national, regional and international levels is essential as, today, no institution can realistically expect to attain the highest standard in every field by itself. Furthermore, the steady advance of information and communication technologies must facilitate inter-university co-operation. Society as a whole must in a democratic system support education at all levels. Mobilization for this purpose depends of the awareness and involvement of Parliaments, the media and governmental and non-government organizations.

Plan of Action

Based on the principles, observations and recommendations set out in the Declaration of Higher Education approved by the Conference, and considering that strong support is needed for the renewal of systems through new policies and new paradigms for higher education founded on such concept as *sustainable development, lifelong education, globalization of knowledge, continuity of the reform process, anticipatory capacity, transparency and accountability, involvement of Parliaments and the media, and preservation of cultural identity and values,* the following is recommended:

Joint Action Plans must be established, in order to prevent duplicated efforts, to optimize efficiency and to ensure the further development of higher education through the enhanced mobilization of additional resources, by international and regional organizations dealing with inter-university co-operation and strengthening of global networks, by all regional, sub-regional and national associations of universities and higher education institutions, by the representatives of private and public universities, by networks of institutions for research and teaching, as well as by development organizations and agencies, governmental and non-governmental organizations. The United Nations University and, in particular, the Institute of Advanced Studies in Tokyo, should co-operate with higher education institutions of the region in strengthening networks and in building global networks leading to the solution of pressing global problems of human survival and welfare. The mass media of the region should be called on to support these initiatives.

Governments and Parliaments must fulfil their commitments to higher education and be accountable for pledges made at regional and world conferences over the past decade with regard to the provision of human and financial resources. This includes, inter alia, the establishment of effective new mechanisms to dead with policy and legislation, appropriate follow-up activities, monitoring and evaluation of progress towards the achievement of stated and the promotion of institutional autonomy.

Each higher education institution must define its mission in harmony with the overall goals of the sector itself, translate this mission into observable indicators and allocate the required resources. The culture of evaluation should thus be established or strengthened in all institutions. These plans of actions should be based on the principles mentioned above and on the principles and considerations of the Declaration approved by this conference and on the proposals stated in this plan of action.

UNESCO, through the join efforts of Headquarters, PROAP and other regional offices in Asia and the Pacific and specialised agencies such as the International Institute for Educational Planning (IIEP), and in co-operation with other UN agencies such as the Economic and Social Council of Asia and the Pacific (ESCAP), must reinforce the programmes of higher education in Asia and the Pacific, including its contribution to the development of the whole education system and, in particular, must reinforce its Unit in Higher Education at its Bangkok Office, so that this may:

- carry out studies, analyses, projects and research activities to support the elaboration of public policies and other initiatives related to higher education in the region. In particular, UNESCO should sponsor a regional process to explore the possibility of developing a framework for quality assessment to feed into the 1998 UNESCO World Conference on Higher Education in Paris;
- provide a venue for the discussion of issues, current problems, long-term challenges and opportunities related to higher education in the region;
- foster training for leaders and senior managers of higher education institutions in the region;
- function as information centre the supports both the work of research groups and of the academic community in the field of higher education in Asia and the Pacific, as well as that of civil society, the state and the productive sector;
- co-ordinate the implementation of the UNITWIN/ UNESCO Chairs Programme in the region and, in particular, to stimulate the development of regional centres of excellence, through the creation of thematic

or geographical networks (with special attention given to networks for innovation, for the utilization of new technologies and for distance education and also for studies on higher education issues);

- work in partnership with regional institutions, associations and networks;
- act as a regional clearing house for inter-country information on higher education institutions and systems in Asia and the Pacific.

The elaboration of plains and decisions taken by the organisations mentioned above should be based on the principles stated below:

RELEVANCE

Major social problems of humankind

1. Higher education must give every student the philosophical, historical, psychological and anthropological foundation of knowledge with regard to humankind, its environment and its different societies. In addition, the motivations, aspirations, transactions and achievements of different peoples within the context of their respective histories and cultures must be communicated.
2. Higher education must support research and pilot curriculum projects which provide expertise to facilitate access to modern technology and scientific discoveries, but which also lead to the understanding, appreciation, internationalization and dissemination of human and societal values, with special attention to the goals of peace and democracy and the protection of the environment.

Responsibility towards other education levels

3. Higher education must act on its responsibility and role towards other levels of education. This is needed not only to ensure that students are better prepared for higher education, but also to bring to bear the resources and expertise of the higher education community to the tasks

of teacher training, socio-economic research on such education variables as school retention and repetition, appropriate pedagogies, and educational policy alternatives, thereby improving education at all levels.

Regional integration

4. Higher education institutions must promote processes aimed at regional integration. Furthermore, cultural and educational integration should be the bases for political and economic integration. In a global environment, higher education institutions must approach their studies on regional integration in the light of the specific economic, social, cultural, ecological and political aspects involved.

Access

5. Governments must expand and diversify opportunities for every citizen to benefit from higher-level skills, training, knowledge and information which are the qualifications for entry into the world of work. Serious efforts should be made to increase participation rates in higher education. Appropriate strategies should be taken for increasing the participation of disadvantaged groups, including women, who must be encouraged to undertake higher degrees and enter academic and graduate employment. Similar efforts are also needed to encourage the participation of ethnic minorities.

The world of work

6. Higher education institutions should promote continuous and interactive partnerships with the productive sector using both reactive and proactive approaches. They must adjust the curriculum to meet the needs of the workplace and ensure that new disciplines and specializations are incorporated into its content. Also, they must help shape the labour market on one hand by identifying, independently of conjunctural interests of enterprises, new local and regional needs, and on the other hand by designing mechanisms for retraining and career-switching. Curricula should be organized to stimulate the entrepreneurial skills

of students. This requires flexible, innovative and interdisciplinary approaches.

7. Countries should create 'observatories' to monitor changes in the labour market in order to facilitate the elaboration of national educational plans and to improve the capacity of higher education institutions to align their policies with national priorities. Special attention needs to be given to career prospects and job conditions of students in course areas of high skills such as engineering and technology for long term development.

8. Governments, the productive sector and local communities should, based on experience gained within and outside the region, encourage institutions of higher education to foster incubator projects which help create new enterprises. Governments, in particular, should provide incentives for the creation of micro-enterprises and fostering of university-industry links.

9. Greater emphasis should be given to the regionalization of specific disciplines, through programmes which target specific needs that will generate employment. In addition, more industry-based projects and new paradigm of university-industry partnership must be instituted, specially in developing countries. UNESCO, UNIDO, UNDP, World Bank, other regional development banks and other funding agencies must be sought in these activities.

10. Innovative approaches such as those of community colleges need to be encouraged. In countries with a large affiliated college system, specific attention needs to be given to strategies for improvement of colleges. Special efforts are needed to strengthen programmes to assist under-privileged groups in society.

Autonomy

11. Responsible institutional autonomy should be stimulated in the region. This principle upholds the freedom to select staff and students, to determine the conditions under which they remain in the university and select research topics.

Freedom to determine the curriculum and degree standards and to allocate funds (within the amounts available) across different categories of expenditure are other aspects to be respected. At the same time, institutional autonomy should be accompanied by a high level of responsibility and accountability.

Quality

12. Appropriate, and if so required, greater emphasis needs to be placed on the renewal of the curriculum, on new approaches to both classroom and distance education teaching, on interdisciplinary and multidisciplinary studies and on vocational education programmes as alternatives to traditional university courses. Innovative approaches to higher education, such as community colleges, international collaboration, and twinning arrangements, need to be encouraged as appropriate.
13. The experience of certain countries regarding the creation of co-operative research centres linking higher education institutions, government research laboratories and industry should be the subject of case studies, the results of which should be available to all countries in the region.
14. Pedagogical programmes should be established to encourage students to be more entrepreneurial and initiative-oriented.
15. UNESCO along with other intergovernmental and non-governmental organisations specialized in higher education must carry out a series of case studies on the region's priorities in the field of higher education. These can include, inter alia, strategic management and planning, interaction among all levels of education, the revision of programmes and training, strategies to enhance the participation of women in higher education and in decision-making bodies, and the development of distance education schemes. Distance education and Open Learning provide important alternative mechanisms of higher education access and learning. In particular, such approaches provide opportunities for those already in the work-force to upgrade

their competencies and knowledge levels. The possibilities of these approaches for school leavers, however, needs further analysis and experimentation.

16. Each country of the region should establish a mechanism for evaluating the quality of its higher education institutions. Countries must introduce quality assurance methods at both institutional and systemic levels. These may include academic accreditation, academic audits and institutional evaluations, performance funding, review of disciplines and professional areas, qualifications frameworks and competency-based approaches to vocational education and training.
17. Each higher education institution should establish a teaching and learning resource unit staffed by qualified personnel and charged with the development of pedagogical skills and other forms of teaching-support activities.
18. Countries and institutions must stimulate, through the creation of networks, the development of regional postgraduate studies.
19. Governments and institutions of higher education must adopt appropriate strategies for the recruitment of staff, for their further professional development and for the recognition of their achievements. Governments, Parliaments and institution of higher education should pay particular attention to the draft Recommendation concerning the Status and Conditions of Higher Education Teaching Personnel, approved recently by a governmental experts meeting, which will be submitted to the General Conference of UNESCO in November 1997.
20. Higher education institutions must provide orientation and counselling, remedial course, study skills training and other forms of student support, including measures to improve their living conditions.
21. Higher education institutions must modernize libraries and scientific equipment and include measures for the purchase and replacement of scientific equipment in their long-term management plans.

22. Higher education institutions must adopt new approaches for the packaging of information, for course delivery, and for rethinking traditional approaches to teaching and learning. The utilization of multi-media, CD-ROM, the internet and interactive video is necessary to promote interacton between students and their lecturers. Agreements should be stimulated among regional institutions to exchange programmes and to organize joint debates and symposia.

23. Teachers, professors and technical and administrative staff must be given training that enables them to integrate new information and communication technologies (NICTs) into their teaching programmes, and to examine the multiplier effect with regard to their use. Frequently, the staff development needs of technical and administrative staff are not properly approached.

Management and Finance

24. Governments must formulate national action plans to enhance both access to and the relevance and quality of higher education institutions. As a consequence, institutional management should improve. The concept of higher education as a public asset implies that its appraisal cannot be restricted to economic quantitative indicators alone. These plans must foresee a diversification of funding sources through, in particular, the encouragement of various income-generating activities, such as contract research, a broad range of academic and cultural services, short-term courses and, if so appropriate, the operation of scientific and technology enterprises. Public support to higher education remains essential to ensure its educational, social and institutional missions. Therefore, the state should take the main responsibility for funding this sector. But, since the challenges for higher education concern society as a whole, the solution to this problem must involve not only the state but all stakeholders—students, parents, the public and private sectors, local and national communications, authorities and academic

association, as well as regional and international organizations.

25. Where appropriate, governments should consider creating, or reinforcing, agencies to act as a buffer between ministries and higher education institutions and to provide advice on resource needs and allocation, regulatory frameworks and the administration of grants and financial assistance.

26. In countries where privatization is accepted, governments should provide a legal framework to regulate institutions, to develop appropriate accreditation and monitoring mechanisms, and to ensure academic freedom and maximum autonomy. The complementary and supportive role of private universities and colleges must be recognized.

27. Management capacities should be strengthened by, inter alia, the recruitment of new senior staff with specialized expertise, appropriate training and staff development programmes for all line managers (and especially for those in executive positions), the introduction of greater clarity in job descriptions and reporting channels, improved management procedures, and the introduction and enhancement of computerized management systems.

28. At the regional level, an association or forum should be created to mobilize the contribution of student organizations to current efforts aimed at making higher education institutions more forceful, active and efficient partners in the promotion of sustainable development in Asia and the Pacific.

29. Staff involvement in decision-making bodies should be considerably strengthened through greater recognition of their needs and by taking into consideration their perspectives, which are often relevant to the analysis of problems and to the search for viable solutions. In the case of students, appropriate consultation is of great importance.

30. Countries of the region must renew the commitments made by them at the Social Development Summit in Copenhagen and at other world bodies to "make new and additional resources available" and thus effectively

increase their budgets allocated to education in general and to higher education in particular, measured as a significant percentage of their gross national product.

Co-operation

31. Individual institutions must develop international linkages, such as those for the exchange of staff and students and for academic co-operation. As well, they must support the activities of international organizations and bilateral agreements between countries within the region.

32. International and regional organizations should support projects aiming at establishing or strengthening university networks. For their part, institutions of higher education—with the support of national, regional and international organizations dealing with inter-university co-operation—should network centres of excellence which respond to the most pressing training and research needs of the Asia and Pacific region. The transfer and exchange of knowledge and experience between higher education institutions, carried out in a spirit of solidarity, should be the basis for these initiatives. It is recommended to establish an evaluation of existing networks in the region, including those covered by the UNITWIN/UNESCO Chairs Programme.

33. In the framework of the Regional Convention on the Recognition of Studies, Diplomas and Degrees in Higher Education in Asia and the Pacific and the International Recommendation on Recognition of Studies and Qualification in Higher Education, there is need to encourage student, academic and professional mobility to benefit the process of economic, educational, political and cultural integration within the region and to develop mutually accepted standards for the recognition of credentials. This will need collective effort by governments, professional bodies and international organizations.

34. Each institution of higher education, as well as all professional associations, must envisage the creation of specialized units for managing international co-operation.

35. Higher education institutions should strengthen their endogenous and co-operative capacities related to priority issues in the region. In particular, centres of excellence can have a positive impact on the solution of major social problems related to the environment and sustainable development, on research in higher education institutions, on educational research in general, on institutional leadership, staff development and teacher training, on the diffusion of new communication and information technologies, on human rights and democracy, on technology transfer, on patents and intellectual property and on the protection of cultural heritage, as well as on the strengthening of education for all and of social development in general.
36. Attempts should be made to develop under the leadership of the Asia and the Pacific distance and multi-media education network under AUAP a general pool of programmes of study for Asia and the Pacific region to cut the cost of distance education.
37. Within their capacity, UNESCO and other international and interregional governmental and non-governmental organizations should respond to the request to provide technical assistance to smaller and poorer countries in the region, in particular those of Island nations, and to collaborate with them in the preparation of joint plans of action with a view to the development of higher education institutions.

7

Europe

A European Agenda for Change for Higher Education in the XXIst Century: Results of the European Regional Forum as a Contribution to the UNESCO World Conference on Higher Education[1]

Preamble

In the framework of the preparation of the 1998 UNESCO World Conference on Higher Education, the Association of European Universities (CRE) and UNESCO's European Centre for Higher Education (CEPES) organized the European Regional Forum in Palermo that brought together almost 400 University leaders, teacher representatives and students, representatives of public authorities and the world of work, and intergovernmental and non-governmental organizations interested in higher education and its development. The Conference was prepared on the basis of twenty case studies of how European higher education institutions of different types and from different regions are addressing the issues of teaching of learning, preparation for the world of work, advancement of knowledge through research, and the transmission of cultural values in a European and a global context, as well as of how they intend to deal with these issues in the future.

1. Palermo, Italy, 24–27 September 1998.

A further input for the discussions was provided by a comparative analysis of these case studies. The keynote address entitled "Europe in a Period of Mutation and Change—The Role of Higher Education" focused on the future role of higher education from the point of view of a large industrial concern, underlining the importance of lifelong learning and the importance of graduates with both professional skills and broad personal competencies. A panel of stakeholders added its comments.

The discussions were based on these various inputs organized around the four case study themes while taking into account the four main dimensions of the World Conference on Higher Education, namely relevance quality, internationalization, and finance and management.

European Agenda for Change—Main Directions

I. Mission

No chain being stronger than its weakest link, higher education should be a strong part of a strong educational system, as well as play a key role in opening new futures by contributing, in close collaboration with other partners, to the innovation chain. Similarly, higher education institutions have a key role to play in European society by contributing to equitable and sustainable development and to the culture of peace. They should act critically and objectively on the basis of rigour and merit, actively promoting intellectual and moral solidarity by serving individual needs. In a world of in-depth transformations, higher education institutions are expected to act responsibly and responsively. They are to foresee, anticipate, and influence changes in all quarters of society and be prepared and able to differentiate and to adapt accordingly.

II. Teaching and Learning

General Assumptions

Given the growing individual demand for higher learning and the resulting pressures on higher education institutions, there is a need for ever more institutional diversification, for new policies of access to higher education, and for a structured development of lifelong learning. In order to better respond to the needs of diversification, a wider and more imaginative institutional profiling is expected to occur within higher education systems, thus leaving less room for categorization of institutions. At the same time, more programmatic diversification within the institutions is required.

Lifelong learning for personal and professional development, for career change, transferable skills, and matching supply and demand for highly trained personnel is essential. Higher education institutions must be able to offer corresponding courses in continuing education and in alliance with employers and other social partners so as to ensure that they are widely available and contribute to a coherent system of higher education. Thus it is essential to define the links in the overall "educational chain" and the relations between them so that individuals can independently manage their learning at whatever level.

In response to this increasingly differentiated demand, coherence means flexibility with regard to: access, content, breadth, depth, and duration of programmes, means of delivery, examination, and validation. Thus, new policies of access should be designed on the basis of merit and equal opportunities, expanding student profiles, and reaching out to hitherto underprivileged groups of society.

Higher education institutions should pay increased attention to promoting strategies for the conceptualization and the management of educational innovation, particularly with reference to organization of contents, learning materials, teaching methods, and graduates' personal profiles as a response to the multiple challenges of their environments.

Required Action

The shift from teaching to learning implies self-managed learning, a coaching role for the teacher, professional support services, investment in new delivery, and quality assurance mechanisms, especially in off-campus operations. It should also lead to a new definition of scholarship balancing discovery and transmission as well as the integration and application of knowledge. A crucial lever for change is a creative and well-defined personnel policy which opens up teaching as a career, supported by appropriate staff development programmes. Particular attention should be paid to the promotion of opportunities for women, including in top positions in higher education.

It also involves a new approach to curriculum development taking into account multi- and interdisciplinarity and flexibility of choice, but in a coherent system which allows for modularization, credit transfer, the validation of work experience, and the organization of the academic year in semesters both at national and international level.

Modern information and communication technologies have major implications for the provision of education and training and require a fundamental restructuring of the ways in which teaching and learning objectives are delivered. Higher education institutions have a key role to play in exploiting, for themselves and together with other partners, the potential of innovative information and communication technologies for academic development.

Given the increased demand for higher education and its democratization, there is a pressing need to share good practice and to ensure academic quality standards by incorporating a culture of quality and the instruments for quality assurance at both systemic and institutional level.

The new roles both of the teachers and of the students as well as the changing relationship to government and world of work imply the definition of a new and explicit "educational contract" between the different partners, setting out rights and responsibilities for all concerned. It will be especially important to ensure that the voice of the students is heard at all stages of the learning process.

The paradigmatic shift from teaching to learning requires and investigation of the desirability of establishing a

European Centre for Teaching and Learning to act as an observatory of good practice and innovation bringing together higher education institutions and their stakeholders at local, national, and international level.

III. Research

General Assumptions

Research, seen as the process leading to the systematic development of new knowledge, is central to the effectiveness of all higher education, while the type of research and the resources and time allocated to its promotion may vary according to the mission statement of the institution and its position within a coherent system of higher education. Accordingly, uniformity of research missions should give way to differentiated institutional policies focused on achievable and competitive performances.

Research is important for the contribution of higher education to the innovation chain, by a strategic mobilization of multilateral co-operation between city and regional governments, higher education institutions, industry, and business. In addition, it contributes to a constant supply of qualified young researchers. At the same time, a strong link between research and teaching opens opportunities for involving good researchers in the teaching process.

Multi- and interdisciplinary research is required more and more to solve pressing societal problems, thus also contributing to sustainable human development. There is, however, increasing concern about the ability of the public purse to provide adequate finances to meet these escalating needs.

Required Action

To ensure continued high quality research, governments need to provide adequate funding for basic research infrastructure, but within a competitive framework. Research funding allocations should be based on quality criteria and transparent auditing procedures. Care should be taken to avoid a mismatch between stockholders' needs for interdisciplinary research and governmental/peer processes of research, audit, and funding, which may be focused on single disciplines. Research in the social sciences and the humanities should not be neglected.

Support mechanisms at national and international level to stimulate and sustain research groups in less developed systems of higher education should be strengthened in order to support institutional development rather than exacerbating brain drain phenomena.

Institutions are encouraged to develop *Codes of Practice* together with their partners for resolving questions of intellectual property regarding the results of externally funded research. Similarly, *Codes of Ethics* for the choice and conduct of research projects should be elaborated.

Strategies for diversifying funding sources should be actively sought. Institutions attracting research funding in this way should ensure that their services are realistically costed and priced and that a percentage of this extra income is used to build up an internal development fund for emerging projects or poorly funded areas.

Networking with corporate laboratories, multinational corporations, especially at regional level, has a particular role to play in enhancing the quality and scope of institutional research as well as its resource base.

IV. World of Work

General Assumptions

In a labour market which is dynamic and heterogeneous, universities should not base their long-term orientations on labour market or manpower planning, but on social demand. They therefore have to prepare their students for meeting the challenges of an intrinsically uncertain labour market. In addition to their professional qualifications, graduates require a broad set of attributes in terms of personal and transferable skills and competencies in order to increase their employability in a knowledge society.

Required Action

To sustain a well-rounded individual development, full participation of stakeholders, in particular representatives of students, teachers, the world of work, and public authorities in higher education policy formation, and curriculum development is essential. As intelligent providers, higher education institutions need to develop their knowledge of markets, anticipate needs, be aware of competition, and invest in processes of quality assurance.

Students have to prepare for an increasingly diversified market, from employment in large industrial concerns to small enterprises, from working in the public sector to the service sector, and not forgetting individual entrepreneurship. There is a special need for the promotion of more constructive relations of higher education institutions to the world of small and medium size enterprises as the sector employing the largest number of graduates.

Higher education institutions should provide systematic information in schools and enterprises to guide student choices, provide placements as an integral part of degree courses, and offer research training in a work environment, as well as career guidance services at all times.

V. Transmission of Cultural Values in a European and Global Context

General Assumptions

Higher education institutions are as much concerned with the creation as with the transmission of cultural values. Although it is misleading to speak of "European" values *per se,* in the specific European context and in terms of the European university tradition, a framework does exist in terms of cultural unity through diversity. They means agreeing to disagree in order to pursue open, critical, and constructive dialogue.

As a consequence, higher education institutions have a key role to play, not only as centres, but also as incubators of cultural diversity and of multiracial harmony and understanding. This means they have a particularly important role to play in creating a civil society and in preparing young people for shaping and living in a democratic society, a place where higher education plays an active role in public debate on ethical and policy questions.

Required Action

These values should permeate all higher education curricula; their transmission, especially as far as ethical considerations are concerned, should not be limited to special courses. Special emphasis should be placed on language training, multi-disciplinarity, and independent and critical learning associated with teamwork. With the help of higher education institutions, this process should start in primary and secondary education.

Attention should be paid to incorporating the European dimension as an integral part of teaching and research and of sustaining the diversity of the learning experience through student and staff mobility. This means strengthening existing provision for the recognition of degrees and diplomas, in particular through the implementation of the UNESCO/ Council of Europe joint Convention, and supporting the further development of a coherent credit transfer system. Furthermore, all efforts should be made to remove practical, administrative, and legal obstacles to academic exchange at institutional, national, and international level. In this respect, the importance of networking and true international partnerships for co-operation in teaching, research, or service is paramount.

VI. Organizational Change and Development

A constructive partnership between government, business and industry, and higher education institutions is a critical element in the implementation of an *Agenda for Change in Higher Education.* The role of government is expected to shift from bureaucratic control to policy steering, stable funding formulae, quality monitoring, project-based investment, and providing a cushion against the wider excesses of the demands of the free market. Business and industry should be encouraged to define more clearly their needs as clients and to work together with higher education institutions as training providers. Higher education institutions should be entrusted with a greater institutional autonomy, thus enhancing their capacity for change, for acting responsibly, effectively, and entrepreneurially as "learning organizations", while making them more accountable in terms of performance. Inter-institutional alliances should be a substantial lever for institutional change and development.

In view of the common assumptions on trends affecting future university development in Europe, the growing systematization of institutional management is a welcome development as is the corresponding awareness of the need for internal strategic planning and rethinking, both for intrinsic reasons and in response to initiatives from national higher education planners.

8

Latin America and the Caribbean

Declaration about Higher Education in Latin America and the Caribbean[1]

Ratifying the terms of the *Universal Declaration of Human Rights,* which states in its article 26, paragraph 1 that 'every person has the right to education' ... and that 'the access to higher education studies will be equal for all, on the basis of their corresponding merits'. Ratifying, in turn, the contents of the *Convention against Discrimination in Education* (1960), which states in its article IV, that the signatory States commit themselves 'to ... offer all people alike higher education on the basis of a real equality and pursuant to the skills of each individual .....'

Starting by assuming the trends identified in the *Policy Paper for Change and Development of Higher Education,* published by UNESCO in 1995. And on the bases of the studies, debates and reflections on that document that have been performed since that date in the region, which have set forth the recommendation of strengthening equity, quality, relevance and internationalization of higher education.

Taking into account the fact that as we enter the XXI century, and faced with the growth of unemployment, poverty

1. Regional Conference on Policies and Strategies for the Transformation of Higher Education in Latin America and the Caribbean, Havana, Cuba, 18–22 November 1996.

and misery, mankind must actively address the following issues: growth with equity, the protection of the environment and the peace-building process. Furthermore, following the recommendations made by the United Nations, via: (a) the *Programme for Peace,* that contains principles and suggestions bearing on the preventive measures that will protect peace, as well as effective actions for restoring peace when uncontainable conflicts emerge, and (b) the *Programme for Development,* that sets forth the conceptual bases for fostering a sustainable and permanent human development.

Highlighting that human development, democracy and peace are inseparable elements—as stated in the medium-term strategy of UNESCO (1996-2001), that aims the higher education programmes of the Organization at three objectives: expanding access to higher education with no discrimination whatsoever, as well as expanding permanence in the system and the possibilities of having success; improving its management and strengthening the links with the labour work; while at the same time contributing to build peace and foster a development founded on justice, equity, solidarity and freedom.

Taking up the report submitted to UNESCO by the International Commission on Education for the Twenty-first Century. The latter, in fact, does not only reaffirm the above mentioned options. It also sets forth that the universities of developing countries have the obligation of carrying out a research that can help solve the most serious problems that those countries are suffering. This is due to the fact that 'they are the ones that should propose new approaches for development, so that they can build a better future and do so in a more effective manner.'

Acknowledging that economic and social development highly depend on training a highly skilled staff, specifically in this most special stage in history, characterized by the emergence of a new production paradigm based on the power of knowledge and the adequate handling of information. Acknowledging, in turn, that it depends on the potential to create a knowledge that satisfies the specific needs and lacks of the region, and that the latter is derived almost solely from higher education institutions—the knowledge instances that generate, criticise and disseminate it.

Accepting, on the one hand, that the gap that is currently setting aside the countries of the region from the developed nations, is evidenced-among other aspects-in the following elements: education (rates of third-level schooling), technological research and development (size of the scientific and technical staff, investment in R&D), as well as information and communications. In fact, these aspects are set forth in the *Report on Human Development of the United Nations Development Programme,* that was published in 1996. Likewise, accepting, on the other hand, that the source of R&D in almost all the countries in the region is public and that the highest percentage of research units operates within the framework of universities, as set forth in the *World Report on Science* published by UNESCO in 1993.

Warning that, without adequate higher education and research institutions, developing countries can not except to adopt and apply the most recent development. And warning, likewise, that it would be even less feasible for them to make contributions of their own to development and to close the gap that keeps them away from industrialized nations.

Taking due note of the fact that higher education in the region evidences the following trends: (a) an outstanding expansion of the student roll; (b) a persistence of inequalities and difficulties when attempts are made at democratizing knowledge; (c) a relative restriction of public investments in this sector; (d) a fast-paced increase and diversification of institutions that work in the field of third-level education; and, (e) a growing participation of the private sector in the composition of the education offer.

Estimating that efforts have been made by higher education institutions, the governments of some Latin American and Caribbean countries, or else, the societies themselves of several countries that make up the region, aimed at increasing the rates of post secondary education. And further estimating that, despite those efforts, many of these nations are still far from achieving the coverage and quality required by globalization, regionalization and economic opening possesses, as well as from achieving a real democratization of knowledge.

Specifying that theses trends are also evidenced at an international level. And, further, specifying that they coincide with simultaneous, though sometimes contradictory processes, namely: internationalization, regionalization, polarization, democratization, isolation and fragmentation, that have an effect on the development of higher education. And specifying, in turn, that the burden of the foreign debt, the increase in the value of imports of goods and services, the drop in the share of world trade, are elements evidenced in the region leading to a situation of social inequality. Furthermore, specifying that the countries of the area make attempts at facing the latter problems with regional and sub-regional groups and implementing several social policies.

Highlighting that, in these times of economic, political or social change-both positive and negative in nature-higher education is called to take up a leading role and to critically study these changes, while at the same time making prospective efforts aimed at predicting and even conducting them via the creation and dissemination of the pertinent knowledge. And, further highlighting that, to this end, higher education must take up its own transformation with the help of society as a whole, not only that of the education sector alone.

Reminding that in the case of Latin America, the Cordoba Reform (1918)—though responding to the needs of a society that was completely different from our own—was characterized by its clear support to the movement of university democratization. Reminding, in turn, that it insisted on the need to create solid and diversified links between university activities and the needs of society—a process that is currently re-emerging to guide the process of transformation of higher education that is underway in the region. And, further reminding that the latter is seen as a continuous phenomenon aimed at designing an original institutional scheme adapted to satisfy the current and future needs of their countries.

Pointing out that any attempt at improving the quality and relevance of higher education requires a significant transformation of the education system as a whole. Furthermore, pointing out that the solution of the financial problems faced by higher education in Latin America and the Caribbean will not stem from redistributing the scarce resources that are allocated to the different levels in this sector. Likewise, pointing out that, on the contrary, they will be the result of transferring resources of other sectors that are not a real priority, while at the same time improving the distribution of income and diversifying financing sources. Pointing out, in turn, that all this has to be the result of a search undertaken with the participation of the State, the civil society, professional and business communities in order to respond—jointly and equitably—to the needs of the different sectors that make up society.

The participants of the Regional Conference of UNESCO on *Policies and strategies for the transformation of higher education in Latin America and the Caribbean,* coming from 26 countries, and assembled in Havana, Cuba, from November 18 to 22, 1996, do hereby declare that:

1. Education, in general, and higher education, in particular, are essential instruments for facing up with success the challenges posed by the modern world and for educating citizens that can thus build a more open and fair society. It will be a society based on solidarity, respect for human rights and the shared use knowledge and information. At the same time, higher education is an unavoidable element for social development, production, economic growth, strengthening the cultural identity, maintaining social coherence, continuing the struggle against poverty and the promotion of the culture of peace.

2. Knowledge is a social asset that can only be generated, transmitted, critized and recreated for the benefit of society, in plural and free institutions that have a full autonomy and academic freedom. However, the latter must also have a clear awareness of their responsibility and a will of service that cannot be turned down. Hence, they will be prepared to search for solutions to the demands, needs and lacks of society. This is indeed a society it should be accountable to—as a requirement—in order to exercise fully its autonomy. Higher education will be able to fulfil this important task only if it demands itself the highest quality. In this respect, a continuous and permanent assessment is indeed a most valuable instrument.
3. Higher education must strengthen its capacity to perform a critical analysis, to anticipate and to have a prospective vision. It must do so in order to prepare alternate development proposals and face the emerging problems of a reality undergoing a process of continuous and rapid transformation, in a long term horizon.
4. Higher education institutions must adopt organizational structures and education strategies that render them highly dynamic and flexible, thus enabling them to respond with both the timeliness and anticipation needed to creatively and efficiently face an uncertain future. They are called to facilitate an exchange of students between institutions and between different degree courses of the same institution. They will have to take up—without any further delays—the paradigm of permanent education. They will have to turn into pertinent centres for facilitating professionals to be up to date, duly retrained and reconverted. Hence, they will have to offer a solid training in the basic disciplines, along with a wide diversification of programmes and studies, intermediate diplomas and links between courses and subjects. Likewise, they must endeavour to ensure that the activities of extension and dissemination are an important element of the academic life.

5. The nature itself of contemporary knowledge—in a process of constant renewal and most sudden and dramatic growth—fully agrees with the current notion of permanent education. This must be an indissoluble supplement of studies aimed at obtaining degrees and titles. They offer graduates the possibility of taking refresher courses and of adapting to changing realities that are very difficult to anticipate. Besides, permanent education should also enable any person—at whatever stage of his/her life—to go back to the classrooms and to find in them the opportunity to be a part of the academic life once again. In this way, people are allowed to attain new levels of professional training. In fact, the competence acquired has a value in itself that goes beyond the mere credential.
6. Higher education must implement pedagogical methods based on knowledge, in order to train graduates that learn how to learn and how to undertake. In this way, they will be better prepared to generate their own jobs. They might even be able to create production entities that can help combat the scourge of unemployment. There is a clear need for promoting the spirit of inquiry. Hence, the student will have the tools to search for knowledge in a permanent and systematic manner. In turn, this implies revising the pedagogial methods that are currently in effect and the emphasis now placed on the transmission of knowledge will switch to the process for generating it. In this way, students will count on the instruments they require in order to learn how to learn, how to know, how to live together and how to be.
7. A changing society demands people to have a comprehensive, general and professional education. The latter must encourage the development of a person as a whole and should favour his/her personal growth, autonomy, socialization and the skills to turn the assets that perfect it into elements having real value.
8. A higher education system will be fulfilling its responsibility and conscientiously carry out its mission—thus turning

into a profitable social element—if a part of its teaching staff and institutions also performs intellectual creation (scientific, technical and humanistic) activities. The latter, in turn must be in agreement with the specific objectives of the institution, its teaching capabilities and its material resources.

9. It is absolutely necessary to introduce a solid culture of information in the higher education systems of the region. The adequate combination of information and communication redefines the need to update pedagogical practices at a university level. Besides, its players need to participate in the major academic networks and have access to the pertinent exchange with all the related institutions. Likewise, they must increase their degree of opening and their interactions with the international academic community. At the same time, higher education institutions must take up the main task of preserving and strengthening the cultural identity of the region. In this way, the above mentioned opening will not endanger the cultural values that are typical of Latin America and the Caribbean.

10. Among the challenges posed by this turn of the century, higher education is now facing the need to participate resolutely in the qualitative improvement of all the levels of the education system. Its most concrete contributions can be made a reality via: training teachers; transforming students into active agents of their training; promoting socio-educational research into problems as could be the case of early school drop-out and repeating; and ensuring its contribution to the design of State policies in the field of education. Every higher education policy must be comprehensive and must address and take into due account all the components of the education system. Most specifically, it must do so under the umbrella of an 'education for all', as set forth in the Conference of Jomtien (Thailand, 1998)—at a world scale—and in the Main education project for Latin America and the Caribbean—at a regional level.

11. Higher education institutions of our region must instil in their graduates the awareness that they really belong to

the community of Latin American and Caribbean nations. Hence, they must promote processes aimed at regional integration. Furthermore, cultural and educational integration should be the bases for political and economic integration. Faced with the formation of new economic spaces within the current framework of globalization and regionalization, higher education institutions must address their studies of Latin American integration in the light of their economic, social, cultural, ecological and political aspects, among others. This will be their main task and they should address the problems with an interdisciplinary approach.

12. Founded on the *Regional convention and the international recommendation* on validation of studies, degrees and diplomats, there is a need to encourage academic and professional mobility. The purpose is no other than that of favouring the process of economic, educational, political and cultural integration of the region.

13. Both the transfer and the exchange of experiences between higher education institutions—key elements of the UNITWIN/UNESCO Chairs programme—are indispensable for promoting knowledge and ensuring that the latter is applied to encourage development. Interuniversity co-operation can be further facilitated by the constant progress evidenced in the field of information and communication technologies. In turn, it can be strengthened by the current economic and political integration processes, as well as by the growing need for a real inter-cultural understanding.

14. The considerable expansion of different types of networks and other instruments and mechanisms for linking up institutions, professors and students is a key issue in the collective search for equity, quality and relevance in higher education. This is specifically the case now, when no institution can hope to master all the areas of knowledge.

15. Public support for higher education is still indispensable. The challenges faced by higher education are also challenges

for society as a whole. They include governments, the production sector, the labour world, the organized civil society, academic associations, along with regional and international organizations that are responsible for the training, research, development or financing programmes.

16. On account of all the considerations above, all the social players must combine efforts and start acting so as to foster the process of in-depth transformation of higher education. To this end, they must be based on a new 'social consensus' that enables higher education institutions to be better positioned and thus have respond to current and future needs for a sustainable human development. In the immediate future, this aspiration will gradually turn more concrete, as the action plan designed in this Conference will be executed.

Plan of Action for the Transformation of Higher Education in Latin America and the Caribbean

Introduction

Any attempt to transform the Latin American and Caribbean higher education systems and institutions (HEIs) must take into account the fact that due to their origins, history, location and fundamental objectives, they present a great diversity which must be recognized and dealt with. Hence, the institutions require particular strategies in accordance with their stage of development and their future goals. Consequently, the process furthered by UNESCO since 1994 through its Regional Centre for Higher Education in Latin America and the Caribbean (CRESALC) has focused on the promotion of comparative research, the provision of spaces of dialogue, reflection and debate among the principal actors of higher education in Latin America and the Caribbean, and the gradual achievement of a consensus as regards strategic guidelines and regional objectives which can help the institutions in the management of their particular transformation.

Among the activities carried out by UNESCO particularly worthy of note is the *Regional Conference on Policies and*

Strategies for the Transformation of Higher Education in Latin America and the Caribbean, held in Havana, Cuba, in November 1996. In its preparatory phase over 4,000 persons connected with higher education and government of the region were mobilized, by holding 36 meetings at the national and subregional level. The wealth of documents generated both by the preparatory seminars and by the Conference itself, which was attended 688 individuals, constitutes the most important source of information available on the problems, challenges and possibilities of higher education in Latin America and the Caribbean today.

The principal documents stemming from that Conference—the 'Final Report', the 'Declaration on higher education in Latin America and the Caribbean' and the 'Guide for the formulation of a Plan of Action'—emphasize and discuss the nature of higher education as a social asset; highlighting its nature as on instrument which is 'irreplaceable for human development, production, economic growth, the strengthening of cultural identity the maintenance of social cohesion, the struggle against poverty and the promotion of a culture of peace'; and assume most of the principles defended by UNESCO in its 'Policy Paper for Change and Development in Higher Education' (1995) and in the General Introduction to the Regional Conference drafted by CRESALC (1996).

The participants in the Regional Conference requested CRESALC to prepare a Plan of Action for the transformation of higher education in the region, which must include common aspects of the national plans and promote inter-institutional interaction and collaboration at the regional and subregional level. The Plan of Action must serve as on instrument of facilitation and catalysis which con bring together in a coherent way the studies and experiences carried out in the HEIs of Latin America and the Caribbean.

The document presented here is the result of a process of consultation and concerted action which CRESALC launched to fulfill that mission. It incorporates the recommendations of the Regional Conference of Havana and contains the input of several workshops held after said Conference, which were attended by government officials responsible for higher education policies, experts in this field and representatives of the non-governmental organizations (NGOs) of the region. It also received the contribution of the professionals of CRESALC and of the UNESCO-Caracas Office, the Director of the Department of Higher Education of UNESCO and the members of the Advisory Group of CRESALC.

Its basic purpose is to outline guidelines which can help to integrate the multiple activities carried out in the region and promote co-operation between institutions in order to increase their efficacy and efficiency, avoid unnecessary duplication of efforts and raise new financial resources. Likewise, the assistance of the various actors and institutions is sought for furthering the changes to meet the challenges posed by adjustment policies, the opening of the economies, the globalization and regionalization processes, increasing poverty; human migrations, vulnerability of democracies, and the collapse and ethical values, which appear as distinctive signs of the end of the millennium in the region.

In order that this be feasible, it is necessary to achieve the proactive and concerted action of governments, parliaments, HEIs and their constituencies, the majority of social actors (workers, entrepreneurs, NGOs) and international organizations interested in improving the capacity of the societies of the region to cope with the aforementioned challenges. The Member States of UNESCO, through their governments and parliaments, with the active participation of the HEIs and within the framework of the new dialogue which we propose, must help to formulate and strengthen educational projects aimed at coping with the needs and challenges identified in their respective countries, ensuring the necessary human, material and financial resources for their uninterrupted education.

Higher education needs to be considered as an integrated system, comprising various sub-systems in constant interaction. Among these, one has to acknowledge the existence of a constellation of university institutions and other HEIs (technological institutes, polytechnic schools, institutes of high studies, technical-professional centres, institutes for the training of teachers, etc.). Each institution must define its mission in harmony with the objectives of sustainable human development, and fulfil its substantive functions using the available resources as efficiently as possible. At the same time, it must provide students with a professional training with a sound ethical and general basis.

It is expected that this Plan will also help to orient action on the part of the international co-operation in order to strengthen the regions capacity to understand and overcome the principal problems of higher education.

1. Fundamental Aspects

Latin American and Caribbean countries are undergoing rapid processes of change which have led to important modifications in their political, economic and social structures. Extraordinary advances are taking place today in terms of technological, scientific and productive capacity, but at the same time, profound inequalities are observed in the levels of progress and development in the various regions of the world.

An international context market by what has been called globalization has given rise to both opportunities and difficulties for Latin American and Caribbean countries. In the past few years they managed to improve their economic growth rates, control inflation, achieve a certain monetary stability, adjust their fiscal accounts and establish democratic regimes. But on the whole, they were unable to occupy a larger space in international trade, nor were they able to achieve a significant reduction of the persistent levels of poverty and social inequality. Hence new strategies are sought today to cope with the challenge of a really sustainable and socially equitable economic development in which priority is assigned to the maximization of the capacities of all human beings.

The region is not alone in this quest, for the benefits of development seem to be concentrated more and more in a limited sector of the world's population, and profound and growing gaps are witnessed in terms of the standard of living and access to the economic and cultural assets between the different social strata, both in the industrialized and the developing countries.

HEIs can be of the utmost importance for the achievement of a new strategy of economic and social development. There is a broad consensus that the future of countries will depend to a large extent on their capacity to maximize the generation of new knowledge. The capacity to create, adapt and adopt new technologies constitutes a strategic element for the achievement of greater collective well being, as well as increased competitiveness of the region and the improvement of its possibilities of insertion in the world economy. Hence the expectations to which universities, technical and professional institutes and other tertiary institutions are subject today require the redefinition of policies, plans, programmes, guidelines, curricula, management capacity and, above all, a commitment to innovation and profound broad-scope transformation.

Knowledge—generated mainly from academic spaces—and technological/productive innovation are of fundamental importance for the achievement of a new stage of economic development, productivity and competitiveness. In order to achieve a better integration between the programmes of higher education and those of science and technology, both in research and in the transfer of knowledge, it will be necessary to reorganize academic and scientific research structures in all areas and at all levels and eliminate the present isolation and fragmentation. It will also be indispensable to allow for scholarly exchange between disciplines and link the projects of transformation of higher education to the needs of the whole society, including those of the social and private productive apparatus. Likewise, the series of demands and needs arising in the region will call for a true reappraisal by the HEIs of the institutional contends, methods and forms, enabling greater flexibility and capacity to respond to the challenges of regional and subregional integration, and to the overgrowing higher education demand.

It is also necessary to reappraise the dialogue between the State and the HEIs, particularly universities, in terms of the emergence of other important actors and of processes which impair excellence in higher education. Only a consensual strategy, in which each entity commits resources and efforts, will enable the necessary transformations. The transformation is more likely to be successful, if it is generated from within the HEIs themselves that if it is imposed or simplistically based on alien institutional models. The challenge lies in the reinvention of institutions in order that they satisfy the demands and deficiencies of Latin American and Caribbean societies, preserving the wealth of traditions, the cultural values and the great diversity and creativeness of their people.

It is important to emphasize that the debate on the transformation of higher education requires a framework, conditions and guarantees, as well as a creative and plural environment to share ideas and reach a consensus as regards strategies of change. In this respect, responsible autonomy is a necessary condition which must be ensured and increased. This condition requires an adequate level of financing by the State, enabling, as a counterpart, the fulfilment of the purposes and objectives of each institution. Within this framework, access to a higher education of quality and its permanence must be ensured for meritorious individuals coming from the less privileged social sectors; in this way the HEIs country be contributing to the achievement of greater social equity. To achieve these objectives remedical or adequate policies could be required to correct the eventual deficiencies of certain social groups.

II. Conception and Objectives

This Plan provides a frame of reference for various types of actions and is aimed at achieving general objectives common to the region. Five major programmes are suggested here, defined on the basis of the main subjects studied in the Havana Regional Conference on Higher Education.

For each Programme, general and specific objectives are identified and principal lines of action are suggested which will enable the development of specific projects by the HEIs, NGOs, international organizations, and governments—key actors in the process of transformation—which will be responsible for taking these proposals to a more specific and operational level.

The objectives and strategic lines of action contained in this Plan will be inserted in the preparations, discussions and follow-up of the World Conference on Higher Education, convened by UNESCO for the month of October 1998.

A. General Objective

To achieve a profound transformation of higher education in Latin America and the Caribbean, in order that it become an effective promoter of a culture of peace, based on a sustainable human development founded on justice, equity, democracy and liberty, improving, at the same time, the relevance and quality of its teaching, research and extension functions, offering equal opportunities to all by means of a permanent education without frontiers, in which merit is the basic criterion for access, within the framework of a new regional and international co-operation.

B. Specific Objectives

1. To generate the bases and conditions for the higher education of the region, in these times of cultural, economic, political and social changes, to assume a leading role in the critical analysis of those changes and in the effort of provision and even conduction, by means of the creation and transmission of relevant knowledge, assigning, to this end, priority to its own transformation and development.
2. To contribute to the transformation and improvement of the conceptions, methodology and practices related to:

(i) the social relevance of higher education; (ii) quality, evaluation and accreditation; (iii) management and financing; (iv) the knowledge and use of the new information and communication technologies, and (v) international co-operation, at the institutional, national, subregional and regional level, in all the functions, and areas of activity of higher education.

III. Programmes

In accordance with its specific objectives, he Plan, as a general framework of operational reference, must implement the following programmes progressively:

(a) Improvement of relevance.

(b) Improvement of quality.

(c) Improvement of management and financing.

(d) Academic management of the new information and communication technologies.

(e) Reorientation of international co-operation.

This set of programmes takes fully into account the fact that the 'Declaration of Higher Education in Latin America and the Caribbean' (Havana, November 1996) stipulated the following: 'All the social actors must unite their efforts and undertake the process of profound transformations of higher education, based on the establishment of a new 'social consensus' which places the HEIs in a better position to respond to the present and future needs of sustainable human, development, which process would at once begin with the implementation of the plan of Action conceived in this Conference'. The next meetings to be held in the Caribbean sub-region will in all likelihood serve to further enrich the programme proposed in this document.

The following description is based on the proposals contained in the 'Guide for the formulation of a Plan of Action' (Havana, November 1996), those stemming from the Consultation Meeting with the Non-governmental Higher Education Organizations of Latin America and the Caribbean (Carcas, April 1997) and the workshop of experts convened by CRESALC on 28 and 29 January 1998, specifically to discuss the preliminary version of the Plan and polish it. Furthermore, the developments in the region in the field of higher education in the period between the Regional Conference (November 1996) and the drafting of the present Plan of Action (February 1998) were taken into account. Evidently, many of the strategic guidelines to which priority has been assigned in this Plan for a programme can overlap with those of other programmes. The intention is, precisely, to stimulate initiatives which have a greater capacity to disseminate and create systemic synergy in favour of an integrated process of transformation.

These programmes will serve as frameworks of action for each of the agents interested in the transformation of higher education in the region to identify the respective projects.

A. Programme of improvement of relevance

According to the contents of the *Policy Paper for Change and Development in Higher Education* (UNESCO, 1995), 'Relevance is considered particularly in terms of the role of higher education as a system and of each of its institutions towards society, as well as in terms of the latter's expectations with regard to higher education'. The relevance of higher education refers to the capacity of the educational systems and of the institutions to respond to the needs of their locality, region or country, and to the demands of the new world order, with diverse outlooks, instruments and modalities. In this plan of action the institutions are called upon to make the necessary changes to ensure greater relevance of higher education.

1. General objectives

1.1 To guarantee that education in general, and higher education in particular, will be essential, instruments, of strategic value, to cope successfully with the challenges of the modern world and to form citizens capable of building a fairer and more open society based on solidarity, the respect of human rights and the shared use of knowledge and information.

1.2 To ensure that higher education will constitute an effective, and at the same time an irreplaceable element for social development, production and economic growth, and for the strengthening of cultural identity, the maintenance of social cohesion, the struggle against poverty and the promotion of a culture of peace.

2. Specific objectives

In order to achieve these aims, projects and activities will have to be designed and implemented which will lead to the achievement of the following specific objectives:

2.1 To guarantee that higher education institutions can become or be consolidated as plural and free entities which, in accordance with the respective national legal systems, enjoy full autonomy, and which, deeply aware of their responsibility, show an unwaivable will to serve in the search for solutions to the demands, needs and deficiencies of the society; to which they must account, as a necessary condition for the full exercise of autonomy.

2.2 To facilitate the capacity of the higher education institutions for critical, anticipatory, and prospective analysis, enabling them to cope, from, a long-term, horizon, which the challenges of a reality subject to rapid and continuous transformation.

2.3 To make changes in the organizational structures and in the educational strategies in order to achieve a high degree of renovation and flexibility in the curricular offer, teaching programmes and methods, providing students with a permanent education of excellence, borderline research, the spirit of investigation, intellectual creation and integral training.

2.4 To induce the region's higher education institutions to take up the challenge of participating resolutely in the qualitative improvement of the educational system at all levels, resorting, among other measures, to the training of teachers; the transformation of students into active agents of their own training; the promotion of socio-educational research, and the contribution to the formulation of State policies in the educational field.

2.5 To help higher education institutions to stimulate in their graduates an awareness of belonging to the community of Latin American and Caribbean nations, promoting the processes which lead to regional integration, and making cultural and educational integration a founding block of political and economic integration.

2.6 To promote research and interdisciplinary studies on the processes of globalization, regionalization, Latin American and Caribbean integration in their economic, social cultural, econological and political aspects, as the basis of programmes of inter-institutional co-operation and collaboration at the regional level.

3. Strategic lines of action

3.1 To promote studies, provide permanent follow-up and propose a solution to the problem of access and drop-out on the part of the poorer sectors.

3.2 To design instruments to increase the linkage between pre-school, elementary and secondary education and higher education, and between, the different sub-systems.

3.3 To promote innovations in the teaching systems, the programmes and curricula, enabling the active participation, personal transformation and full development of the potential of each student.

3.4 To stimulate research and the exchange of experiences related to educational innovations, enabling the accumulation and evaluation of experiences.

3.5 To implement new study programmes which in the medium term ensure a universal post-secondary education of quality. It is proposed that short careers be designed which increase the possibilities of insertion in the labour market and which, with a view to updating skills education, enable the continuity of studies.

3.6 To encourage the creation of postgraduate courses, programmes of non-formal education and updating courses which make lifelong education a reality.

3.7 To design plans for the dissemination of results and experiences of the HEIs, showing clearly the social and economic benefits which they contribute, for the purpose of facilitating their evaluation by society and promoting support from new social actors.

B. Programme of improvement of quality

According to the aforementioned UNESCO Policy Paper (1995), 'quality embraces all its main functions and activities: quality of teaching, training and research, which means the quality of its staff and programmes and quality of learning as a corollary of teaching and research ... the search for quality ... It therefore also implies attention to questions pertaining to the quality of students and of the infrastructures and academic environment ... Finally it is essential to indicate that the principal objective of 'quality assessment' is to achieve institutional as well as system-wide improvement'.

1. General objective

To guarantee the complete and prompt adaptation of higher education to what it must be, bearing in mind that the quality of higher education is a multidimensional concept, which includes universal and particular characteristics related to the nature of the institutions and of knowledge, and to the problems which arise with regard to the different social contexts within the framework of national, regional and local priorities.

2. Specific objectives

In order to achieve this general objective, projects and activities will have to be designed and implemented enabling the achievement of the following specific objectives:

2.1 To ensure that the quality of the systems, institutions and programmes of higher education is essentially linked to social relevance, to the preparation and commitment of professors and researchers, to the social responsibility involved in the work of the institutions, and to their accountability vis-à-vis the society with regard to their global performance.

2.2 To identity mechanisms to ensure that higher education recovers its roots as an indomitable patrimony, in a globalized world in which the mass media affect the national, subregional and regional cultural identities.

2.3 To initiate forms of interconnection between higher education and the other subsystems, in order that they cope jointly with their problems, and to collaborate in the design and implementation of solutions, in the understanding that the quality of higher education is, moreover, contingent upon the rest of the educational system, with which it interacts.

2.4 To construct the quality of teaching fundamentally on the basis of the improvement of acaαemic training and an integrated training in the design and development of curricula, in order to provide creative, thoughtful, polyfunctional and enterprising graduates, within the framework of systems of advanced, continuous, open and critical training, in which the students assume their role as active subjects, actors of their own learning, and managers of their life project.

2.5 To further the consolidation of common multinational academic spaces for the development of subregional or regional postgraduate studies, the implementation of co-operative research, and the edition of joint publications.

2.6 To achieve a culture of evaluation of performance which, by means of different strategies ranging from self-evaluation and self-regulation to state accreditation, will enable the systems and institutions to achieve their fundamental objectives and strengthen responsible autonomy.

2.7 To promote the creation of mechanisms enabling, on the one hand, the financing of the costs of evaluations and, on the other hand, the allocation of the necessary resources to solve the problems detected in the feasible projects presented by the institutions themselves as a result of evaluation.

2.8 To obtain, in the short, medium and long term, an improvement of the educational service by assimilating the technologies of computer science, telematics and distance education and by placing the merits of the teaching activity on the same footing as those of research and extension.

3. *Strategic lines of action*

3.1 To promote regional postgraduate studies, in particular around issues of strategic values to the region.

3.2 To facilitate the exchange of students and the insertion of graduates of different specialities in the labour market, based on the results of the accreditation experiences of each country.

3.3 To promote integral plans for the training of teachers and researchers, ensuring their full dedication to academic life and institutional development.

3.4 To make a great effort to introduce the culture of evaluation, ensuring the most extensive participation of the academic community and the dissemination of results in order to reflect, and guide the institutional policies, and to guarantee the fulfilment of objectives and goals of each institutional programme.

3.5 To maintain the principle of voluntary support of the process of evaluation in the institutions which enjoy autonomy.

3.6 To promote evaluations of a formative nature, both in the institutional aspect and in the tasks performed by students and teachers, in order to improve the quality of their academic performance.

3.7 To consider the international aspect in the processes of evaluation, taking into account the needs and possibilities of co-operation between institutions.

3.8 To create mechanisms for financing costs of evaluations and to overcome the deficiencies identified, in the event that such deficiencies exist.

3.9 To increase the use of the new technologies of computer science for innovation and pedagogic experimentation and the strengthening of access to information and documentation resources.

C. Programme of improvement of management and financing

In order to achieve the objectives of relevance, quality and equity of this Plan of Action, a significant improvement of the managerial capacity and the level of financing of the HEIs will be required, within the framework of a joint effort on the part of the whole society. At present, the management of an HEI, particularly that of the most complex ones, encompasses not only the administrative aspects, but also the governmental and academic aspects. Since the investment in education in the region is below the level agreed upon by governments themselves, and in view of the current requirements of an education of excellence, measures must be taken to increase the level of resources, diversify their origin, achieve a better distribution among institutions, and increase the efficiency of expenditures.

1. General objectives

1.1 Bearing in mind the unavoidable responsibility of the State in the financing of public higher education, to contribute to the improvement and transformation of management capacity of higher education by means of the adoption of appropriate policies and the diversification of its sources of financing. Strategies to this end are needed in all areas and levels of activity, supported by research on higher education.

1.2 To develop strategies aimed at stressing the importance of higher education as a key sector for the economic and social development of Latin America and the Caribbean, helping higher education institutions to obtain official support in the quest for sources in addition to public financing and achieving greater flexibility in the use of public funds in accordance with the objectives of the respective allocations.

1.3 To produce the necessary orientations for the strategic and anticipatory management of higher education institutions to help the system fully identify the current changes and future trends and adapt to the speed with which the phenomena occur in different areas.

2. Specific objectives

2.1 To promote comparative studies and research on management and financing of higher education experiences at the national, subregional and regional level, in order that the institutions establish and finalize explicit policies in the field.

2.2 To favour the formulation of models of allocation of resources which take into account specific objectives such as quality, equity and balanced regional development from the point of view of the actors of the programmes of higher education and to validate their use in negotiations with multilateral development and financing organizations and with national financial institutions.

2.3 To design and propose new systems of financing of the HEIS via the national financial institutions.

2.4 To formulate new models of management of systems, institutions and financial resources for higher education in the region and establish a permanent action of formation and intensive training of directors and administrators to contribute to the adoption of flexible and transparent management practices.

2.5 To ensure that the new models of academic management combine research and postgraduate activities with undergraduate ones, in order to facilitate social integration, extension and transfer of knowledge.

3. Strategic lines of action

3.1 To favour a State policy for the distribution of incremental resources based on specific programmes or projects presented by the institutions which can be financed, bearing in mind the need to ensure transparency in the allocation, control verification, and dissemination of results.

3.2 To achieve commitment of the part of the State to pluri-annual programmes of financing of higher education, ensuring the fulfilment of goals and objectives.

3.3 To identify, in accordance with the respective national legislation, possible complementary sources of funding, which can be obtained by means of new taxes, incentives to donations to the HEIs or taxation of certain financial transactions. The institutions themselves must carry out studies and research to quantify the potentiality and viability of these proposals.

3.4 To promote by adequate means the marketing of the products, services and technological developments generated by the HEIs, projecting intellectual property and collaborating in the management of patents and certificates.

3.5 To design flexible systems to facilitate collaboration and the sale of the services of HEIs to public and private organizations in projects destined to overcome needs, deficiencies and demands of the society.

3.6 To promote an efficient management of national and international co-operation in order to take better advantage of operating capacities.

3.7 To further new mechanisms of student scholarships and/or loans, particularly to poor ones, in order to facilitate their academic performance.

3.8 To favour the creation of various types of incentives to reward excellence and productivity of both teachers and officials.

3.9 To introduce new administrative techniques which increase rationality in decision-making, including the preparation of budgets, allocation of resources and the implementation practices, in order to increase the transparency and control of management. To develop training programmes and monitoring to that end.

3.10 To promote flexible administrative entities in order to ensure the concept of lifelong education, in programmes of non-formal education, training, re-skilling of workers, teaching of adults, and co-operation with trade unions, among others.

D. Programme of academic management of new information and communication technologies

The new telematic technologies are opening up extraordinary possibilities for higher education but they also raise serious questions regarding the very functioning of the institutions. The possibilities of immediate interaction and exposure to vast sources of information which they open, necessarily modify the inputs, processes, and products of higher education as we have known them. Hence, it is essential that a perfect understanding be achieved of how the region can use, generate and adapt the new technologies to improve the quality, relevance of, and access to higher education without running the risk of generating an even greater difference between social sectors and between countries, in terms of the capacity to handle these new tools.

1. *General objectives*

1.1 To produce pertinent policies and strategies to base the social and economic development of the countries on, among other factors, knowledge and use of the new information and communication technologies (NICT).

1.2 To induce the region to make the necessary investments for an adequate infrastructure of telecommunications and teleinformatics, enabling flexible and cheap connections to the global networks for the HEIs, favouring access to INTERNET, and the promotion of INTRANETS.

1.3 To achieve the integration of the new technologies by the HEIs in all the areas of their work.

2. *Specific objectives*

2.1 To formulate policies which assert the right to information and communication as a central element of an education for all, without exclusions.

2.2 To achieve the development of a Latin American network for higher education and the consolidation of the national university networks.

2.3 To strengthen a culture of exchange, collaboration and academic work by means of electronic networks and to succeed in having these serve as a vehicle to disseminate the cultural values of Latin America and the Caribbean.

2.4 To modermize higher education in all its aspects—contents, mythology, management, and administration—by the rational use of the NICTs. Likewise, that the HEIs consider these new technologies as an object of study, research and development.

3. *Strategic lines of action*

3.1 To establish national and regional systems of information, with data bases and statistics regarding the priority areas of common academic interest, taking into account especially the particular needs of the Caribbean region.

3.2 To organize presential and virtual training for teachers, researchers, students, and administrators, in order to ensure the full utilization of the NICTs in higher education.

3.3 To explore the creation of postgraduate studies of excellence on priority subjects by means of collaborative consortia among institutions of the region, making use of the possibilities offered by work in networks and distance education.

3.4 To further the creation, via the NICTs, of HEI consortia in the region for major research projects which require resources and critical mass beyond the capacities of one single institution.

3.5 To promote the creation of centres of excellence in the production of multimedia for teaching activities, information services and the preservation and dissemination of the Caribbean and Latin American cultural patrimony.

3.6 To strengthen the academic networks and other mechanisms of liaison between institutions, professors, and students, since few institutions can dominate all the areas of knowledge, for the collective quest for equity, quality and relevance for higher education.

3.7 To identify the centres of excellence in NICT, stimulate their work through a network, and help to disseminate their experiences.

E. Programme of international co-operation

International co-operation has been an important mainstay of the Latin American and Caribbean HEIs. Nevertheless, it has also served sometimes to support foreign models of generation of knowledge, curricular construction, views, methodology and work styles. On the other hand, there has been an evident flow of financial resources from the South to the North and, in many cases, instead of contributing significantly to the strengthening of the systems of education and of science and technology of the region, the co-operation has brought about an important and sustained emigation of professionals and scientists with high levels of academic training from the region to the industrialized countries. In this new historical context, it is important to promote relations of mutual learning and greater horizontality. Many institutions of the region have accumulated valuable experiences which can be transferred to other institutions via new systems of international co-operation, seeking to reduce the existing asymmetries.

1. General objectives

1.1 To redirect international co-operation to the strengthening and maximization of the intellectual, cultural, scientific, technological, humanistic and social capacities of the region by means of the development of higher education and science and technology.

1.2 To overcome the existing asymmetries, within a new framework of collaboration, assigning priority to a logic of solidary integration which overcomes the differences and leads to work in priority areas with shared resources and proactive horizontal structures enabling the launching of innovative programmes of research, teaching and social projection.

2. *Specific objectives*

2.1 To ensure that inter-institutional co-operation is facilitated by the constant progress of the information and communication technologies and strengthened by the current processes of economic and political integration, and by the growing need for intercultural understanding.

2.2 To ensure the transfer and exchange of information and experiences between HEIs-essential elements of the UNITWIN/UNESCO Chairs—in order to promote knowledge in favour of sustainable human development in the countries of the region.

2.3 To ensure support of governments, HEIs, NGOs connected with postsecondary education, and the Latin American and Caribbean inter-university networks, to the UNESCO International Institute of Higher Education for Latin America and the Caribbean which is being established.

2.4 To stimulate academic and professional, mobility in favour of the economic, educational, political and cultural integration of Latin America and the Caribbean, based on the Regional Agreement and the International Recommendation on the accreditation of studies, degrees and diplomas.

2.5 To increase the presence of higher education within the framework of UNESCO's activities in the region and strengthen the links in this field between Latin America and the Caribbean.

2.6 To promote the learning and use of the different languages of the region in order to, improve the quality of academic and cultural exchange.

3. Strategic lines of action

3.1 To design a system whereby information regarding the total operating capacity of human, scientific and managerial resources in the Latin American and Caribbean HEIs is easily available, which can serve as a basis of programmes of regional inter-institutional cooperation, and to keep it permanently up to date.

3.2 To strengthen the entities of exchange of information and experiences between HEIs in terms of the ideal of regional integration.

3.3 To extend and help to consolidate the work of the networks of horizontal co-operation in higher education already existing in the region, as well as that of others which may emerge, and to promote exchange between them and other regions of the world.

3.4 To facilitate academic mobility (teachers, researchers and students), emphasizing the recognition of partial studies, degrees, diplomas, based on flexible mechanisms of accreditation.

3.5 To favour the launching of specific horizontal co-operation projects and the signing of agreements enabling better use of the physical resources and the human capital.

3.6 To create postgraduate networks enabling the training of teaching and scientific personnel in the HEIs which do not have this type of infrastructure and the reformulation of shared programmes recognized at the regional level.

3.7 To form new university networks like the AUGM in other subregions as soon as possible, and a programme of scientific and technological academic strengthening by launching megaprojects like those of the European Union.

3.8 To prepare personnel specialized in the management of horizontal co-operation with the support of international organizations and experts.

3.9 To make rational use of the financial resources available in development agencies and organizations, and in the HEIs themselves.

3.10 To create in CRESALC a focal point for the Caribbean community with a view to an advantageous integration of Latin America and the Caribbean.

3.11 To promote and sustain a programme of development of skills in the use of the languages of the region within the higher education communities, both academic and institutional.

In the course of the different stages of the process of consultation which resulted in this plan of Action, the eminent persons who took part in it, members of both the academic and the governmental domain, deemed it advisable to recommend that CRESALC, as a regional centre of UNESCO, adopt this Plan of Action and that it dedicate all its experience, capacity, creativity and commitment to the progress of higher education to the fulfilment of the objectives and strategic lines of action set forth in this document, making it an instrument for the guiding of its own activity and the orientation of cooperation with the governments and with HEIs in the Latin American and Caribbean region.

Part III

Commissions

9

Relevance in Higher Education

Viewpoints: Venezuela, Nicaragua, United Kingdom, Puerto Rico, Poland

In a rapidly changing social and natural environment, higher education is called upon to play a varied and complex role in development. **Relevance** is a key factor in this regard and this term has been used to refer to the fit or the match between what higher education institutions do and what society expects of them. This concerns the role and place of higher education in society, but it also covers access and participation, teaching and learning, the research function of the universities, the responsibility of higher education to other sectors of society, the world of work and the community service function of higher education.

Factors Affecting Relevance in Higher Education Systems and Institutions

These are:

- the role of Government in higher education
- population growth and population education
- globalization, regionalization and sub-regionalization
- rapid scientific progress
- access and participation
- increased cultural sensitivity and pressure for democracy and peace

- the need to cater for more diverse clienteles and changing labour market needs
- new instructional methods resulting from the application of new technologies
- funding constraints and privatization
- reorganization of systems and diversification of structures.

Improving Relevance

Important challenges include: *constructive partnerships between government and institutional leadership, demonstrating the impact of higher education in development, correcting provision imbalances on the national/regional/subregional levels (including rural/urban provision), promoting institutional diversification as well as innovative curriculum and pedagogy, preserving cultural identities, advancing knowledge through research, and linkages to the whole education system.*

Recommendations

The specific aim of **Relevance** in higher education is to mobilize the responsible actors from the different domains, including politics, universities, science, technology, industry, and business, to build up a strong coalition of all actors concerned, and to establish a permanent dialogue with ministries of finance and other sources of funding.

Recommendations and proposals should address:

- the relationship of higher education to the national development model, contributions to its design and improvement;
- how higher education can contribute to the consolidation of a culture of peace, the preservation of national identity, regional integration and human development;
- relevance as the result of scientific/technological research and its integration in the process of global

development, and the articulation of proposals to guarantee this;

- relevance as response to real social needs and how to achieve this;
- relevance as a support for human resource development; as articulation with the productive sector of goods and services and the economic/ employment sectors; as collaboration with civil society and organized communities at the local level; and as support for the modernization of the State and for political co-operation.

Regional Viewpoints

- Basic Principles for Relevance—Prof. Carlos Tünnermann Bernheim (Nicaragua)

The following concepts relate to the relevance of higher education and should guide national policy-makers in their reforms:

- higher education is a public good; as such it serves society and merits a strong commitment from governments;
- access on merit is a fundamental human right;
- higher education has—and should maintain—its function as social critic;
- its prospective and anticipatory role is unique;
- through its cultural mission, it educates responsible citizens who are aware of global issues;
- higher education institutions have a duty to be socially accountable.

Finally, by concluding a moral pact with governments to promote social development, institutions will help construct a culture of peace based on the principle of learning to live together.

- Changing Patterns of knowledge Production

Prof. Michael Gibbons (Association of Commonwealth Universities)—United kingdom

The rules for the production of knowledge are changing and have three new criteria:

- public and social accountability—the contribution of higher education to national economic performance and to an enhanced quality of life;
- market sensitivity and demand—induced activities—a premium on innovation and on problem-solving;
- connectivity—the capacity to network, to forge linkages, and to establish partnerships.

As the fundamental occupation of universities is being transformed, important questions are:

1. Are we right in our higher education development efforts to place so much emphasis on increasing enrolments in science and technology? Or should we instead be emphasizing curriculum reform to develop the skills needed for effective knowledge production under the new paradigm: team-building, creativity, information management, problem-definition, networking, communication skills, and social sensitivity?
2. Should we not be giving much more attention to building capacities for problem-solving research, and particularly for research management, and less attention to improving the inputs for university teaching?
3. Should we not recognize the fundamental role now played by communication technologies in the process of knowledge production? Consequently, should we not be more aggressive in promoting investment in electronic communication systems, which enable university communities in developing countries to link up with sister institutions and to access global resevoirs of knowledge and information?
4. Should we not be giving less attention to the development of national policy frameworks for tertiary education, and much more attention to the development of national innovation policies?

5. Finally, all of us are products of the traditional university paradigm, and we work on a daily basis with the vested interests concerned with university preservation. How, then, can we possibly play the role of change agents in the field of higher education?

- Diversification: Flexible Systems of study
  Prof. Jerzy Woznicki (Rector of Warsaw University of Technology)-Poland

A flexible system offers the student a variety of opportunities and must be supported by a computerbased organizational infrastructure.

Practical example

- the five-year programme leading to the Master's degree;
- the sequence of two programmes: 3.5-4-year undergraduate programme leading to the Bachelor's degree and 1.5-2-year graduate programme leading to the Master's degree.

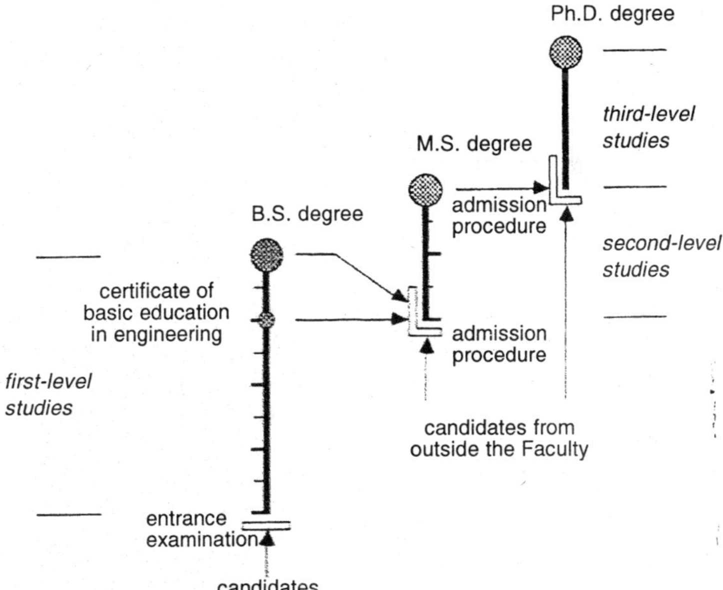

Standard three-level system of study

- Diversification: A Typology of Trends in the North America Region and the Periphery
  Prof. Eduardo Aponte (Puerto Rico Council on Higher Education)

Recent policy efforts to transform higher education in the new context of societal development can be demonstrated by the following selected examples:

Form	**To**
1. Governance and mission	
• decentralized, multi-campus institutions	• differentiated missions to meet student demand, and market-oriented institutions.
• community colleges	• colleges focused on specialized knowledge, the economic sector, population groups and professional needs.
• traditional research/teaching in institutions	• entrepreneurial institutions with modernized management and innovative teaching/ learning research methods.
2. Funding	
• public, private, philanthropic and alummi	• public private and international funding, capital investments from various funding sources.
• proportionate allocations and priority funding	• performance and strategic budgeting.
3. Knowledge	
• basic scientific/social research	• applied research (scientific, technological and social)
• general and specialized knowledge	• production and diffusion of useful and multi-specialized knowledge.
• specialized international studies	• internationalized curriculum and projects for regional integration.

4. Organization development

• academic departments and professional units	• organizations which are: • entrepreneurial and consumer-centred. • flexible and innovative.
• departments/degrees organized by disciplines	• interdisciplinary "clusters" or centres and flexible curriculum.
• teaching and learning in classrooms	• research/learning experiences in other settings (e.g. internships and community projects).

5. Evaluation policy

• accreditation based on national norms	• accountability, performance, continuous self evaluation, external audit systems based on results.
• national/regional accreditation	• transnational/regional accreditation agreements.

Points for Further Reflection in Different Contexts

- What are the priority national needs which should be met by higher education?
- What indicators can be established to measure the current and desired relevance of higher education?
- What are the consequences of increased demand for higher education in a given context?
- What are the major problems faced by students and learners?
- Can higher education be further diversified to meet demand?
  (i.e. greater variety of post-secondary provision)
- Can current resourcing problems be better resolved?
- What major obstacles are preventing the transformation of higher education to meet the needs of the 21st century?
- How can relevance and capacity-building for citizenship be harmonized and made complementary?

10

The Quality of Higher Education

Viewpoints: Cuba, Kenya, Canada, Colombia, France

Quality assurance might denote: *"All the policies, systems, and processes directed to ensuring the maintenance and enhancement of the quality of educational provision within an institution. A quality assurance system is the means by which an institution confirms to itself and to other that conditions are in place for students to achieve the standards that the institution has set."*

Quality often means *fitness for purpose,* i.e. that an institution must have in place adequate mechanisms to assure itself and others that it is able to achieve its stated aims and objectives, and that these will be achieved consistently. This recognizes the *diversity of higher education missions and provision; and the importance of the educational process.* It links to *value for money,* which is attractive to governments and other funding agencies, and may be measured in terms of indicators such as failure or drop-out completion rates, teacher to students ratios etc. *Quality assurance is thus associated with increased institutional autonomy accompanied by greater transparency and accountability.*

Other approaches to the concept of quality include:

- *something distinctive or exceptional;*
- *excellence and maintenance of high standards using bench-marking criteria;*

- *an educational process producing a standardized 'quality product' which relies on defined minimum threshold standards;*
- *transformation referring to the enhancement of the abilities of students (adding value as the key objective of the educational process).*

Components of Quality

- Quality is a multi-dimensional concept with no single set of standards applicable to all countries and institutions.
- This concept embraces: governance/management, teaching and academic programmes, research and scholarship, staffing, students, infrastructure, and the institutional environment.
- Quality assurance requires comparisons between observed and intended outcomes, and constant analysis of the sources of dysfunction. Both internal self evaluation and external review are vital components of a sound quality assurance system to demonstrate accountability.
- Quality assessment involves matters of judgement, academic values, and cultural understanding.

Strategies to Enhance Quality

- Fundamental restructuring of the ways in which teaching and learning objectives are delivered including regular curriculum review and ICT usage;
- Strategic alliances with industrial stakeholders for co-operation in the provision of part-time and co-operative/in-company education, and closer linkages with the world of work;
- Flexible exit levels which are qualitatively as high as previously, but consist of carefully pre-defined learning outcomes, competencies, and transportable skills as definitive quality measures, rather than focusing principally on entry standards;

- Innovative management and education delivery underpinned by adequate financial and human resources.

Mechanisms and Structures

Institutional processes must include *mission definition in line with the overall goals of the national education system, observable indicators to implement assessment, internal institutional self evaluation and external peer review.*

System-driven review can be assured by a government agency (e.g. higher education quality council/inspectorate), by a non-governmental association of the institutions themselves (e.g. committee of vice-chancellors), by a combination of both, or by an independent body. They review might be either supportive/formative (emphasizing quality improvement) or summative/evaluative (stressing accountability) or a combination of both.

Some quality assessment system have as their objective academic accreditation, qualifications frameworks, and outcomes and competency-based approaches to vocational education and training.

Increasingly, institutional funding is linked to quality assessment.

Conclusions: Major Concerns Related to Quality

The ultimate aims of quality assurance are:

- *preparing citizens to live in a globalized society*
- *meeting the changing needs of the world of work*
- *safeguarding cultural pluralism*
- *developing adequate management capacities*
- *internationalizing of teaching, learning and research*
- *optimizing the potential of the new information and communication technologies.*

Finally, perhaps the major challenge for systems and institutions worldwide will be evaluating the quality of higher education and training for learners with diverse backgrounds and preparation.

Regional Viewpoints

❑ Alliances with the Employment Sector—A Pre-requisite for Quality
Prof. Miguel Angel Escotet (Cuba)

Quality depends on the creation of stable links between the university and society. Much closer ties with the employment sector will foster a spirit of understanding regarding priorities and forge new partnerships. Such alliances should:

1. *associate basic and applied research with the economic sector*
2. *involve practitioners in teaching university programmes*
3. *make the university a provider of lifelong learning in the workplace*
4. *orient both professors and students towards the reality of the world of work and towards social cohesion*
5. *reinforce social values—a tenet of interuniversity co-operation-in relation to the workplace*
6. *strengthen the role of the university in services and projects which stress the social aspects of the market*
7. *fund projects which recognize the ownership of ideas and innovation*
8. *emphasize the economic rate of return provided by the university via its highly educated and trained graduates*
9. *share scientific and technological resources to improve quality and accelerate the transfer of knowledge and knowhow.*

❑ Innovation in Curricula and Teaching
Prof. Florida A. Karani (Kenya)

Interdisciplinarity—Promoting Quality Higher Education

- Establishment of teaching units and learning resource centres in all institutions of higher learning and training university teachers in pedagogy are desirable, as this will not only contribute to the quality of teaching but will provide a platform for interaction **between disciplines.**

- Fast and rapid change in education, the rise of new disciplines such as computer education, the deteriorating quality of teaching brought about by large numbers of students entering higher education institutions, the information revolution and diminishing financial resources call for the establishment of teaching and learning units.
- **Inter-university computer links** should help to promote interdisciplinary interaction.
- **Interdisciplinary research** is best placed to address developmental problems.
- African universities should establish **networks** for mutual benefit and facilitate inter-university/ interdisciplinary activity.
- **Pilot resource centres** established in selected regional centres should also facilitate inter-university, interdisciplinary activities.
- Training should adopt **thematic approaches** that are problem-solving in orientation (to address development challenges) but which are pertinent across the disciplines in socio-economic, political and scientific contexts.

❑ Transforming Higher Education and Maintaining Quality—Important Components
Mr. Paul Cappon (Canada)

Expectations

Each national or regional system of tertiary education needs to make clear to its constituent institutions a precise set of public expectations, which represent the values and expected outcomes of the system generally and institutions specifically.

Differentiation

A transformed higher education system would promote effective articulation of its different sectors, such that the system becomes a "seamless web" for students transiting it throughout their lives.

Role of basic sciences, social sciences and humanities

The natural sciences, social sciences and humanities remain at the core of the university. These disciplines, and their inherent values, provide skills that are important to employment prospects, as well as to personal growth, social development, and a sense of civic responsibility.

Role to technology-mediated learning in the transformation of higher education

(i) there should be no artificial transition to the use of ICI in tertiary education. The basic tools should be mastered by students before accessing higher education, to ensure a seamless transition into tertiary education.

(ii) Application of technology-mediated learning should become as frequent and effective in core university disciplines as in professional and technical programmes.

(iii) Students should be induced to develop equal levels of comfort with both traditional and technology-mediated patterns of teaching and learning.

(iv) A significant challenge for higher education systems in most countries will be the design of linguistically, socially, and culturally distinctive pedagogical materials for technologically mediated delivery. Otherwise, the probability of international standardization will be high.

❑ Globalization—The Determining Factor in Lifelong Learning
Prof. Luis Enrique Orozco Silva (Colombia)

This phenomenon is now the prevailing influence over all countries and their socio-economic systems. It reiterates the facility and benefits of communication and social harmonization and perhaps homogenization. Underpinning this dynamic is technology which permits the free exchange of ideas and of cultural values. However, this without frontiers is paradoxical:

- it confirms the values of freedom and equality
- it starkly points to the growing inequality of wealth distribution and its social consequences.

Against this background, lifelong learning has become a priority so that people can adapt to social change. Learning, unlearning and relearning are important variations on this same theme. Education can take place at any age, in many varied settings, via diverse delivery systems, through the recognition of experience.

The ramifications for the university are of the greatest importance:

- teaching and learning must be seen as interdependent and complementary; this will replace the classical one-way communication of knowledge and know-how from professor to student;
- equipping the student for this challenge re-opens the old debate on the best choice of course. Here, the value of a sound liberal arts/humanities education is often reconfirmed. Does this, by virtue of its inherent flexibility and variety, provide the best foundation for the many learning unlearning and relearning imperatives to be encountered throughout life?
- a flexible, informed professoriate—also capable of learning, delearning and relearning—and excellent technology support systems will be essential elements of the lifelong learning environment;
- lastly, present institutional structures must change; for instance hierarchical structures and mono-disciplinary approaches must give way to freer and interactive programmes which reflect social reality.

Flexible, diverse, holistic—such will be the characteristics of lifelong learning institutions in the future.

❑ Career Guidance—Service and Responsibility
Mr Jean—Luc Brun (France)

Today, given the nature of the labour market, it is an institutional responsibility to provide career orientation services to students. Advice on courses, their possible openings, and on movement between types to programmes is considered indispensable—and indeed, this is demanded by the informed student contemplating his/her future.

Career guidance has 4 functions:

1. It constitutes a tool to help student choice. In this regard, academics, who orient students, confirm their pastoral role, by virtue of their knowledge and experience.
2. This becomes an information service for the institution and helps confirm its specific mission. Here, co-operation between the administration and academics is essential.
3. This tool facilitates transition between university and the world of work via contacts with future employers.
4. This service promotes equality of opportunity—some students will automatically benefit from family advice regarding career choice; others—perhaps the first in their family to enter higher education—frequently need more orientation.

Points for Further Reflection

- How can national systems and institutions promote and elaborate broad criteria for the definition of the quality of higher education to serve as a base to be adopted by each country according to its national requirements and circumstances?
- What steps are needed to create national and regional systems of evaluation and accreditation for higher education programmes and institutions?

- How can governments be encouraged to allocate fixed national budgets for higher education over a certain period of time in order to ensure adequate planning and high-level quality?
- What strategies can facilitate the exchange of information and experiences with regard to quality improvement practices carried out by different countries?
- With regard to protecting the quality of academic staff, how can the 1997 UNESCO Report on the Status of Teachers be better promoted and utilized?
- What are the qualitative criteria for measuring quality and administrative efficiency in higher education?

11

Management and Financing of Higher Education

Viewpoints: Australia, France, India, Brazil, Macao, Israel

The management and resource challenge is threefold:

- *to diversify and thereby to increase the resource base;*
- *to achieve economies and greater effectiveness by more skilful and more imaginative use of resources;*
- *to gain a wider understanding and acceptance, within the community, of the investment argument.*

Therefore, the challenge to leadership and management is *both within the institution and at the system level.*

Major Trends and Issues

These can be summarized as follows:

- *governance attuned to the complexity of the changing socio-economic context*
- *meeting demand and increased student numbers*
- *more efficient use of human and financial resources*
- *management based on transparency and accountability*
- *questions related to regulation and autonomy*
- *student involvement in decision-making*

- *managing new teaching and learning systems, including ICT use*
- *changes in systemic infrastructure and institutional practice.*

Conclusions

The strategies and methods directed towards support for and reform of higher education are numerous and varied. One essential task is to define, provide and sustain the conditions upon which teaching learning, study, research and scholarship depend. Directions for improving the quality and relevance of academic work fall within this essential task and set criteria for its performance.

Major limiting factors in this process are:

- *low and declining levels of financial resources*
- *the gap between the capabilities of existing personnel and the numerous challenges they are called upon to meet*
- *the persistence of rigid structures and procedures which stand in the way of the flexible and and creative approaches that are so clearly needed.*

Together with the recognition of the urgent need to meet societal expectations and economic requirements, any discussion of management and financing must reiterate the ultimate aim which is a peaceable, democratic and just civil society and international order which provide a beacon for the direction higher education should take.

Regional Viewpoints

❑ New Challenges for Govern nce and Management
Prof. Ingrid Moses (Australia)

Systems

Countries are redefining long-established concepts to:

- *ensure lifelong access to education for all citizens;*

- *balance national goals and institutional autonomy—and satisfy individual aspirations;*
- *determine the funding responsibilities of government, students, business and others;*
- *provide for and balance teaching and training through institutions, private providers and workplace education and training;*
- *situate the university system within a global education system;*
- *guarantee quality.*

Institutions

Issues to resolve are:

- quality education for all in a mass higher education system;
- attunement to regional needs and international collaboration;
- Striving for excellence in research and providing quality education for all;
- collegial structures and accountable executive leadership.

Individuals

Individuals will face the biggest challenge to their status, tenure and must endeavour to balance a wide range of activities.

❑ Changing Resource Patterns
Mr. Bernard Saint (The French University Presidents' Conference)

The French experience indicates that major changes have occurred on the funding front. And, the growing emphasis on the principle of institutional autonomy (in the managerial sense of the term) has obliged both the state and universities themselves to re-assess their links and, in the latter case, to seek alternative sources of financing so as to implement their policies.

Two important changes have taken place in France:

- ***Financing by objectives*** *has recently been established and is linked to the process of contractualization, which has been developed gradually since 1987.*
- ***University autonomy*** *also means a diversification of the funding resources and the capacity of these institutions to obtain increasing levels of self-financing.*

Although remaining faithful to their traditional roles of public service, teaching and research (for which they are the cornerstone), universities must meet the priorities of their particular eras. The change process means adaptation to the local environment and the anticipation of needs. To respond effectively to the challenges of quality and relevance, flexibility of resourcing has become essential.

❑ Global Concerns—Varied Approaches
Dr. Bikas Sanyal (International Institute for Educational Planning)

Main Functions of Financial Management

Acquisition/mobilization of resources, management of cash flows, allocation of resources, utilization of resources, evaluation and auditing.

Strategies for Financial Management

☆ *At National Level*

A sample may include:

Mechanisms for resource allocation, allowance for flexibility in the utilization of resources, creation of an institutional framework (legal or other) conducive to the diversification of resources, generation of new resources via student loans and a discriminatory fee-paying system, development of a private higher education sector, allowance for financial planning at the institutional level, retention of a dominant role of the state in higher education.

☆ ***At the Institutional Level***

Present approaches cover:

Integrated financial management and institutional policies, facilitating income and cost-recovery at the basic unit level (e.g. China, Chile, Jordan, Kenya), reducing costs and increasing efficiency, developing appropriate administrative structures, setting up Management Information Systems (MIS), providing adequate training at all levels of staff.

❑ Public and Private Funding Sources: Conceptual Issues
Dr. G.D. Sharma (University Grants Commission)—India

Public sources

Advantages:
- equity, democratization, promotion of merit and clearly orientated sustainable development

Disadvantage:
- red tape, delays over control causing inefficiency and lack of innovations

Private sources

Advantages:
- immediate need and market orientation
- flexible and dynamic

Disadvantages:
- those who can afford may not necessarily be meritorious
- iniquitous, promoting those endowed with financial resources and perpetuating inequality
- lacking long term and larger public concern and interest

Other private sources

☆ Endowment funding/donations

☆ Sales and services

Advantages:
- may prove to be more efficient and promoting both long and short terms needs of the society

- enhancing social accountability and societal need orientation
- reducing subsidization to rich

Disadvantages:
- lack of certainty of funds
- occasional conditionality and control on governance and serving certain interests

❑ Brazil: Funding—Key Functions and Questions
Dr Wrana Maria Panizzi

Funding strategies reply to 5 key questions:

- *What is the total of resources and how are these spent?*
- *What is the origin of the funding?*
- *How are resources distributed and who are the beneficiaries?*
- *Is higher education perceived as socially relevant?*
- *Who is paying for international co-operation?*

❑ Funding Scientific Research at the University of Macao
Prof. Zhou Li-Gao

The University of Macao, established in 1991, is now offering Master and doctoral courses to strengthen research.

Here the main strategies are:

- ensuring funding via the University Senate;
- sponsoring research projects in the Macao community,
- supporting other research-based entities e.g. *Macao-INESC (Institute of Computer and Systems Engineering);*
- linking to international projects e.g. the *EUREKA Meets Asia* exhibition was arranged with the European Union;
- publishing the *University Academic Journal;*

- guaranteeing status for researchers via a special Charter;
- co-operating with government in R and D via the *Research Grant Application System.*

❑ Prof. Amnon Rubinstein: Diversifiying Higher Education Reform in Israel

The recent Israeli reform aimed to extend access to tertiary education without excessive cost to the state. The main elements are:

- undergraduate enrolment at research universities is limited;
- the majority of undergraduate students will study in academic colleges awarding a Bachelor's degree—the cost of this provision is much lower than research institutions;
- other colleges, non-subsidized by the state, are accredited by the Council for Higher Education; these now enrol 10% of students who pay fees between $2500 and $5000;
- new Engineering Schools—concentrating on training for hi-tech industries—have been established; they award a Bachelor of Technology in Engineering Sciences and ensure registration for the profession. Thus, Israel has doubled the number of trained engineers;
- non-Israeli institutions may sent up branches and charge fees—over 30 such campuses offer sought—after subjects such as law and business.

The reform—initially controversial but now strongly supported—has doubled student numbers since 1990.

Points for Further Reflection in Different Contexts

Governance

- What mechanisms best foster "accountable institutional autonomy"?

- Should the state provide incentives for institutions to achieve specific objectives? Can this be done?
- How can equitable cost-sharing be assured?
- What mechanisms might be effective to improve government/institutional communication?
- How can tertiary institutions provide diversified education and training and, at the same time, remain "research-informed"? (i.e. aware of knowledge creation even if not directly involved therein)
- Based on specific experiences, are universities competitive in relation to other providers in the tertiary sector?

Financing

- How can funding be realistically diversified in contexts of economic instability?
- How can the fundamental missions of teaching, research and community service be protected as private resourcing increases?
- How can fair and equitable methods be devised to identify and assist needy students?
- What strategies may help ensure that well-qualified staff are retained by institutions?
- How can ICT usage reduce costs and enhance access?

Education Credit

- What are the pros and cons of such systems in relation to a specific context?

12

International Co-operation

Viewpoints: Spain, Russian Federation, United States of America, Argentina, the Association of Universities of Asia and the Pacific (AUAP), the Netherlands Organisation for International Co-operation in Higher Education (NUFFIC)

Internationalization—the recognition and implementation of the transnational dimension of higher education—has had 3 phases:

- a ***convergent*** phase during the Middle Ages and Renaissance, when universities had common programmes and international staff and students;
- a ***divergent*** phase (1800 to 1945) when higher education institutions served national interests;
- the current ***reconvergent*** phase where universalism and internationalism are vital concerns.

Important factors are:

- ***globalization*** and ***regionalization*** of economies which privilege knowledge and information. Education is seen as a key component of policies for economic and political integration;
- ***communication and information technologies*** which have radically changed the scope of international co-operation in higher education;

- international co-operation in higher education now addresses the ***exponential growth of knowledge,*** which expands beyond national entities.

Complementary factors are: *student mobility which excludes the South; innovative networking and linkages; and the continuing dilemma of the Brain Drain.*

Issues raised in the regional preparatory conferences

Africa: higher education requires regional and international support. Donor aid remains essential to maintain the functioning of institutions and to halt deterioration.

Asia and the Pacific: a programme is needed to encompass the entire region which has the world's largest student numbers. The Association of Universities of Asia and the Pacific (AUAP) is a key actor is this. The economic, political and cultural diversity requires the inclusion of all institutions and countries.

Latin America and the Caribbean: Inter-American co-operation is strong but LAC universities should expand their international links.

The Arab States

Co-operation prospects are good given the shared cultural heritage and already healthy partnerships with other regions.

The Europe Region

Since 1990, the EU and other countries have been higher education as a force for development and integration. East-West links are solid provided that co-operation is not subject to paternalism from outside sources.

Key Aspects of Internationalization

These are:

- *the rationale of internationalization*
- *defining guiding principles and objectives*
- *expected outcomes*
- *various dimensions of co-operation (bilateral, regional and global)*

- *forms of international co-operation in higher education (i.e. mobility schemes, stemming the Brain Drain, internationalizing curricula/programmes, innovative networking/linking arrangements, research on co-operation, the role of ICTs)*
- *the management and financing of international co-operation (i.e. planning, evaluation, cost-effectiveness, commercialization)*
- *the international equivalence/recognition of qualifications*
- *the potential of partnerships*
- *international co-operation as a factor of development.*

Conclusions

In today's global environment, higher learning and research facilitate the sharing of knowledge so essential for training young people who will occupy leading positions of responsibility in the social, economic political, scientific and cultural life of nations. Higher education can contribute to this through collective action as a world community of scholars, researchers and institutions.

Given the complexity and the increasing costs of international co-operation, higher education institutions must develop their management abilities in this field. These include appropriate mechanisms and strategies for the systematic *evaluation* of and *research* on international co-operation in higher education. Also needed is capacity-building at institutional and national levels, and for IGOs and NGOs which are active in this field internationally. UNESCO should lead this, noting the needs of developing countries.

Regional Viewpoints

❑ Networking for Solidarity, Participation and Knowledge Transfer
Prof. Lorenzo Olarte Cullen (Spain)

The Canary Islands are a tourist destination and a common meeting place for the African, European and Latin American continents.

Students number 50,000 of the 1.6 million inhabitants. Important efforts to diversify and innovate have taken place in the last 15 years. Academic networks are effective for strengthening regional and inter-regional linkages. Co-ordinated by the Universidad de La Lagun and the Universidad de Las Palmas, these focus on important development priorities: Environmental Management, Health, Tourism, and Informatics and Technology. Examples are:

- the ISA Network in Tourism and Sustainable Development with universities in Portugal, Spain, Brazil, Dominican Republic, Puerto Rico, Venezuela, Nicaragua, Peru and Chile;
- a new network for Africa to associate institutions in Mauritania, Morocco, Senegal, Cape Verde, Sao Tome and Principe and Guinea Bissau.

❑ From Brain Drain to Brain Gain—The LINGUAUNI Network
Dr. I. Khaleeva (Russian Federation)

Today, a new paradigm educates individuals who can cope with a constantly changing world in terms of communication, technology and cultural integration. For this, linguistic education, and especially in Russia, is vital.

Linguistic education helps mould the consciousness of the individual in order to make his/her world coherent. It instills in the individual the feeling of readiness for dialogue, respect for native cultures, traditions and languages, and promotes tolerance for these as well as the capacity for cross-cultural communication. Today, foreign language learning:

- *is vital for multinational states*
- *must link language and culture, thereby leading to intercultural education*
- *should promote cross-cultural communication*
- *should met international standards in this domain*
- *should, therefore, ensure the acquisition of clear levels of competence*

- *should benefit from a strong support system for quality control (e.g. certification procedures)*
- *should take advantage of ICT usage for optimal provision.*

These are the objectives of the LINGUAUNI network which brings together some 29 universities in 16 countries in Western and Eastern Europe, China and Japan.

❑ Higher Education Partnerships for Development
Dr Emily Vargas-Baron (United States of America)

As higher education will change greatly by 2010, priority elements are:

- *promoting the number and rate of returnees*
- *optimizing the potential of virtual universities*
- *establishing new bridging initiatives (e.g. Young Professionals for Development, Sabbaticals for Partnerships, a Professor Emeritus Volunteer Corps)*

These strategies will depend on dynamic alliances. How should these function?

Criteria and Steps for Sustainable Partnerships

- balanced, reciprocal relationships are essential;
- all partners should participate in planning, implementation and evaluation processes of the partnership;
- a shared vision must be created that leads to building a relationship of trust;
- the benefits for all partners must be identified, reviewed frequently and achieved;
- an action plan should be developed jointly with responsibilities and timelines for all partners;
- clear lines of communication between partners and their supporters must be established and nourished;
- face-to-face exchange visits including all supporters are essential; email and teleconferences are not enough to sustain long-term commitments;

- concrete partnership programmes should include development activities (e.g. the exchange of curricula, focused research endeavours, internal and external evaluations, community outreach strategies, and similar topics);
- achievements, problems and needs of the partnership must be reviewed periodically by all partners and supporters of the partnership;
- partnerships must be flexible and open to adding new partners, re-prioritizing activities and revising action plans.

❑ The Pros and Cons of International Academic Co-operation
Dr Luis Jalián Lima (Argentina)

International academic co-operation assumes: common interest, mutual respect, reciprocal credibility, solidarity in the production and application of knowledge, support for the concept of "community based on diversity".

Advantages

- quality can be enhanced (provided this is clearly defined)
- association brings benefits for partners
- the academic provision can be diversified
- first cycle study time can be reduced to lead into more varied post-graduate courses.

Disadvantages

- one model of education can dominate other contexts
- the human capital produced can be uniform in character
- information and training can be confused
- the true co-operative spirit is not respected.

❑ Managing Partnerships
Prof. Cary A. Duval (Association of Universities of Asia and the Pacific)

Planning, management and evaluation very important in any co-operative project. The first step is to define areas of mutual concern that a group of universities can most efficiently improve by pooling resources.

The UNESCO/UNITWIN network on Asian Environmental Education with Bunkyo University, Griffith University, Prince of Songkhla, University of the Philippines and Nankai University, the APDMEN (Asian Pacific Distance Multi-Media Forum) and the Bunkyo Foundation Scholarship Fund exemplify this approach.

Essential components are:

1. a strong, efficient, well organized secretariat
2. co-operative sponsors
3. standardized bookkeeping procedures among members to satisfy sponsors.

A co-operative projects must be continually evaluated by a management committee to ensure that it is achieving its goal(s). If not, changes must be made. In short, we must be more businesslike in our approaches. Continual evaluation ensures both financial soundness and relevance to society.

❑ The Importance of Strategic Planning
Dr Jos Walenkamp (NUFFIC–the Netherlands)

Strategic planning is the key to improved institutional development via co-operation in higher education. Elements can include: *a strategic 5-year development plan, an annual rolling plan, community involvement in this process and in the implementation and monitoring phases.*

This is happening in Tanzania, Mozambique, Ethiopia and Burkina Faso where academic pursuits are balanced by planning and management.

First, if institutional development is hampered by inadequate management, this negatively affects North-South academic co-operation. If 25% of and efforts and funds or North-South collaboration were shifted from academic development to reinforce management, the overall result may be better, despite 25% less funding.

Second is the ownership question. A strategic plan formulates a mission statement and then implements. This participatory process involves the whole university community and external stakeholders. The plan is owned by the whole institution. It should be the framework for all developments, including North-South collaboration, so as to:

- eliminate many undesirable aspects of North-South co-operation such as donor dominance;
- be a central force for institutional development and so avoid a tendency to decentralize excessively.

Points for Further Reflection

Principles, Goals and Strategies of International Co-operation

- How can higher education institutions be pro-active and inter-active (rather than reactive) vis-á-vis the processes of regionalization and globalization?
- What are the needs of institutions in the are of international co-operation and how can management capacities be strengthened in this regard?
- How can a Code of Practice be elaborated to ensure ethical conduct in the growing market for international higher education?

Partnerships and Networking

- How can genuinely symmetrical alliances be promoted between institutions of the North and South?
- Aside from institutions themselves, what other partners should be included in these co-operative arrangements?
- What is the potential for an Academics Without Borders scheme? (i.e. academic volunteers)

Academic Mobility

- Can more resources be found to satisfy growing demand in this area?
- Can incentives be offered to guard against the dangers of the Brain Drain?
- To what extent can mobility issues be assisted by the use of ICTs?
- What strategies can facilitate better recognition/ equivalence of internationally earned qualifications?

Part IV

Thematic Debates

13

The Requirements of the World of Work

Viewpoints: Switzerland, Cameroon, Germany, United States of America

At the end of the 20th century, the connections between higher education and the world of work are again among the key issues of debate whenever challenges for innovation in higher education are at stake. The following questions are frequently asked: what is heightening the interest in the connections between higher education and the world of work? How are job requirements and employment conditions for graduates changing? What is higher education expected to "deliver", and how does it and should it respond?

At first glance, experts predominantly observe that job prospects for recent graduates have been bleak in most areas of the world during the 1990s and that the continuing enrolment growth in higher education premises little relief. A closer look reveals, however, that assessments of the situation are not consistently negative and that the prevailing perceptions and views regarding the connections between higher education and the world of work are controversial in many respects. Divergent views persist because systematic information on graduate employment and work is scarce and there are no indisputable criteria for assessing graduate employment. Graduate employment is assessed more favourably when compared to that of non-graduates than when compared to the graduate employment and work situation which prevailed a few years ago. All in all, the signals from the employment system are more blurred and ambivalent than ever before.

It is remarkable, however, that many experts and key actors agree on the main directions in which higher education must head in response to the changing challenges from the world of work. Higher education is expected to:

- continue to consider fair access according to socio-biographic background to be a key issue;
- further diversify structurally and thus as regards conditions of study and courses provided;
- devote greater attention to generic competencies, social skills and personality development;
- reshape its function in the move towards a society of lifelong learning;
- prepare students for the growing economic and societal globalization and internationalization;
- serve students through an increasing variety of means beyond classroom teaching and learning, for example through out-of-class communication, counselling, the provision of various forms of work and life experience or job-search support;
- establish regular modes of communication between higher education and the world of work.

The broadest consensus has emerged with regard to the main directions to head in. There is work to be done on specifying ways and means of overcoming existing barriers and finding promising solutions. The conditions in various regions of the world, cultures and societies, economic systems and stages of economic development, specific sectors of higher education systems as well as various fields, disciplinary cultures and professional areas may thereby require specific solutions.

Furthermore, divergent long-term scenarios also play a role, as terms such as "crisis of the work society", "risk society", "professional society" or "knowledge society" suggest. And last but not least, the institutions of higher education interpret their role vis-á-vis the world of work differently. Readiness to respond to changing demands is widespread as well as concern about instrumentalist pressures.

Most experts agree that higher education must be well-informed of expectations from the outside world in order to adopt the necessary proactive role and thus respond to the need to prepare students for indeterminate future job task, new employment patterns and contributions to innovation in society.

Regional Viewpoints

❑ The World of Work—The Employers' View
Mr. Hédi Djilani (Switzerland)

Preparing people for work is naturally a major concern of the International Employers' Federation which I chair and which has 25 chapters across 5 continents. I also comment as a business man from a developing country, Tunisia.

Two questions must be addressed:

- *should universities continue to expand if, as some think, there are too many students?*
- *how can university education better meet the needs of the labour market?*

These are particularly significant for the developing world where universities remain far too distant from the employment sector. However, employers, as "consumers of graduates" must also shoulder their responsibility by offering work experience to young people. Lack of communication is common: sometimes, the expectations of students and graduates are too high; sometimes, the business sector has an inadequate understanding of a university education.

Tunisia now devotes 35% of the national budget to education. Benefits have included greater equality of opportunity for all, a bigger middle class who values education, adaptation to technology and the attraction of foreign investment. The social success is clear.

However, developing countries must grow stronger in 2 areas: *their capacity to create jobs and to accord executive status to jobs in companies to be filled by graduates.* As globalization is obliging all countries to become competitive, strategies are needed to recognize and reward talented graduates. Using INTERNET for recruitment is one example.

Today, we face an increasingly uncertain labour market where even legislation has less weight. Since there are no guarantees, dialogue between employer and employee and flexibility bring the best results.

Two essential areas for the future are:

- *closer co-operation between the public and private sectors*
- *the safeguard of equal employment opportunities for men and women.*

❑ Preparing for the World of Work: A Student Opinion Ms Sike Nelle Sombe (Cameroon)

Employment, as a primary development issue today, must concern universities and their students. Given the context of the developing world, the question has special importance.

Universities prepare people for life—this is a long-term investment but must include sound professional capacities which can adapt to changing conditions. These institutions must balance theoretical knowledge with practical training. Moreover, they can prepare students for their working lives in several ways:

- students can take responsibility for the management of certain campus facilities;
- internships can be arranged to give students a first-hand experience of their future professional milieu;
- student NGOs in professional domain (such as AIESEC for students in business and economics) should be present on campus to help orient students towards their working lives.

Sadly, certain students are disadvantaged regarding such opportunities—for instance, part-time students and women with children. Such people are aiming to enter the work force after their studies and so institutions need to be much more accessible, via technology and flexible programming.

Certainly the employment question would benefit from much closer co-operation amongst the parties concerned: universities, students, NGOs and professional groups, and policy-makers.

❑ Linking Higher Education and the World of Work: The Trade Union Viewpoint
Mr Gerd Köhler (Germany)

We support UNESCO's position on open access to higher education. But looking at reality, we are asking for more means and clearer political action to reduce social, gender-based, income-related, religious or regional inequality. There are too many seeds without any chance to grow. Access must also be provided for gainfully employed people and mature students who do not hold traditional entrance qualifications to move between labour market and higher education institutions.

Studying means vocational qualification on the level of academic education, but should not be reduced to that aspect along. It must not be geared solely towards the undiscussed requirements of the employment system, but should facilitate a critical insight into a professional world in which graduates from higher education want to find meaningful, humanly conceived and well paid work. We are calling on the higher education institutions to discuss the relations between studying and occupation, between higher education and labour market. The demand for higher education qualified employees should become an issue in a transparent dialogue with both the private and public employers on the one hand, and the trade union on the other.

Further or adult education is becoming increasingly important for economic and social development. The higher education institutions are asked to take their role in the process of lifelong learning. UNESCO's CONFINTEA conference (Hamburg, 1997) has shown the types of activities required and the dimension of this task.

Research forms the foundations for qualified teaching. Therefore the unity of research, scholarship and teaching must be guaranteed as advocated by UNESCO's Recommendation concerning the status of teaching personnel in higher education. Governments must also guarantee sufficient basic funding to ensure that in choosing its topics, higher education research does not have to orientate itself primarily on the criterion of direct of indirect practical application. Research must reflect its responsibility to society in a "code of conduct". Market and trend-driven research will lose its function of critical enlightenment, it will only reproduce "mainstreamism", the opposite of innovation. "Shareholder-value" politics would destroy long-term basic research.

The trade unions demand that working conditions at higher education institutions should be appropriate to research activities. Organisational structures should be created to enable a reversal of the trend towards increasing fragmentation, casualisation and the exodus of research from higher education. Continuity of research work and team work are principal conditions for its quality. And, there can be no innovation without new ways of participation.

❑ Meeting Future Challenges
Dr. Donald Gerth (United States of America)

The World Conference on Higher Education has been the occasion for the education, economic, and government leaders of the world to assess where higher education was, in 1998, and where we need to go in the years ahead. The fact that we need to address the world of work is a product of complex economic and social forces. In the language of educators and others, it is a direct result of a massive shift in the twentieth century to "the substantially rising proportions of graduates" of universities and other higher education institutions. Higher education is no longer for an elite. Higher education is broadly understood, in most places in the world, to be a principal path to employment with economic well-being and a good life. Thus it is only natural that the general population in most parts of the world and their governmental leaders would understand a very basic relationship of higher education to the world of work. Indeed, that relationship is coming to be one of the defining characteristics of a healthy higher education system and even of most, if not all, universities.

The 20th century began with much of higher education in a traditional mode. The work of universities for the most part was to address and transmit knowledge in the traditional disciplines. The advent of applied field and the interdisciplinarity of knowledge were only beginnings. In my country the so-called land grant colleges were in their early years. Many if not most members of the professoriate and many if not most of the universities educated individuals understood universities and higher education in what were then and, in some places, still are traditional terms.

In the early and mind and, in some places, later years of this century, the world of works began to intervene in the functioning of universities. A common and early reaction to this phenomenon was that of forcing a choice. Higher education was to be in the arts and sciences, the disciplines as we have understood them, or to be in vocational areas, applied fields, and both conventional and emerging professions. In some countries, this clear separation was, and in some instances still is, reinforced by the organization of higher education.

As universities and other higher education institutions have matured in terms of the newly emerging economic and social orders of the last half of the twentieth century, gradually there is in fact a coming together of the traditions of higher education and the world of work. But this coming together is often uneasy and hardly accepted. In part this uneasiness is a direct result of the "massification" of universities and higher education, in part the result of a loss of direction for the disciplines in an interdisciplinary world, in knowledge based societies.

The next step is an obvious one, or so it would seem. That next step is for universities to embrace the world of work within institutions that remain as committed as ever to the integrity of knowledge and its dissemination, to research and the arts, and seek interdisciplinarity, the professions and applied fields. These come together, and a university that understands this will create a strength that will maintain it into the future.

The alternative is equally obvious. To insist upon a division is to create in a changing world institutions which are not likely to survive in good health because they are not useful. An educated person in a knowledge-based society is one grounded in the skills and knowledge of civilizations past and present, as well as prepared to function in a knowledge-based society.

Points for Further Reflection

- How can higher education and responsible governments become better informed about employment trends and the work expected from graduates entering a changing labour market?
- How can the world of work learn to appreciate creativity and innovation—which are the hallmarks of university graduates?
- What barriers are preventing this closer communication between academic and the employment sector and how can these be removed?
- How can institutions best prepare students for the new types of "graduate jobs" (e.g. middle-level occupations, self-employment, the service sector)?
- As more students enter higher education in search of qualifications, can a healthy balance be struck between general and specialized education and training?
- How can institutions foster the acquisition of skills as well as knowledge?

14

Higher Education and Sustainable Human Development

Viewpoints: UNESCO, Germany, Côte d'Ivoire, the Netherlands, UNDP, Zimbabwe

A principal mission of higher education today is to prepare future generations for a sustainable future. This has dominated university debate and United Nations' activities subsequent to the Earth Summit (Rio de Janeiro, 1992).

Sustainable human development is a process of change in the relationships between social, economic and natural systems and processes. These interrelationships must reconcile economic and social progress with safeguarding the global life support systems. Universities, and all institutions of higher education, increase our understanding of the issues at stake to lead and develop consistent future scenarios, and increase awareness of problems and solutions via their educational programmes. Universities set good examples themselves at the local and regional levels.

How can interdisciplinary and collaborative research and education programmes be best implemented, how networks of interdisciplinary discourse can be promoted and how staff and students can be encouraged to have an environmental perspective in whatever field of study they are engaged? It is essential to recognize the emerging role of universities in refining the concept and key messages of education for sustainable development, integrating environmental, demographic, economic, social and other concerns inherent in the complex notion of sustainability. However, universities must re-orient their research programmes and curricula for flexible interdisciplinary co-operation and collaborate with institutions outside the university. Changing the way people operate and strengthening their "inner drive" to contribute to sustainable development is more important than changing higher education systems.

In addition to identifying key issues, this debate elaborated a future strategy to close the gap between theory and practice and between ideals and reality to prepare this sustainable future:

- create a "University Platform for a Sustainable future";
- create an electronic network by establishing a major webside;
- establish a sustainable future award scheme;
- develop a "preparing for a sustainable future" audit system;
- start a feasibility study to identify the potential of universities to contribute to the future implementation of Agenda 21;
- establish a special fund for direct mutual transfer of knowledge;
- establish programmes for the training of trainers;
- reinforce UNESCO's work as task manager for Chapter 36 of Agenda 21 and for the International Work Programme of the Commission on Sustainable Development and encourage all actors within the international community as well as at national level to implement this work programme.

❑ A Strategic Vision for Change
Prof. Gustavo Lôpez Ospina (UNESCO)

To change universities, much thinking, discussion, trial and error are required. A few proposals are:

- **The key to the new vision is ethics and values.** We need to rethink higher education through an ethical filter that coincides with the kind of sustainable and equitable society we want for the future.
- An **"international democracy of knowledge"** would move the world towards the future without losing the richness and diversity of cultures. We need to reverse the paradoxical situation where people find that "the information they have is not what they want; the information they want is not what they need, and the information they need is not what they can obtain".
- Ways should be found so that **research** can fully contribute to the quest for a sustainable future; universities can find ways to promote networks and co-operation.
- The **reinforcement of international co-operation** can direct the available scientific knowledge and information towards educational purposes and workable policies for sustainable development.
- Adapting to an era of rapid technological change and globalization should **not compromise the freedom of the academic community to pursue intellectually "pure" thinking and research.**
- **Reorienting the educational system** for new requirements has implications for curricula at all levels of education. But it is not, and cannot be, the task of the educational system or universities to solve all the problems of society. Of critical importance will be the changes in lifestyles needed in all regions and societies.

❑ Higher Education and Local Agenda 21 Schemes
Dr. Peter W. Heller (Germany).

The Local Agenda 21 Programme provides a good platform to "refine the concept and key messages of education for sustainable development" at the local level and to build and improve practical skills in urban planning and management. Higher education relates to all five key elements of the Local Agenda 21 planning process:

- Multisectoral and *interdisciplinary engagement in the planning process* through a local stockholders' group which serves as the co-operation and policy body for preparing a long-term sustainable' development action plan;
- Consultation with community groups, NGOs, business, churches, government agencies, professional groups and unions, in order to raise public awareness, to create a *shared* vision and to identify priorities for action;
- Participatory assessment of local social, economic, and environmental conditions and needs;
- Participatory target-setting through negotiations among stakeholders in order to achieve the vision and goals set forth in the action plan;
- Monitoring and reporting procedures, including local indicators, to track progress, and to allow participants to hold each other accountable to the action plan.

The increasing interest of researchers, lecturers, students and local officials in the Local Agenda 21 Programme has stimulated a number of projects. Among them are:

- the "UN Habitat project" of the School of International and Public Affairs at Columbia University, New York City;
- the Export Seminar "New Public Management of Natural Resources", jointly organized by ICLEI and the London School of Economics and Political Science, London.

❑ Sustainable Development: The Challenge for Africa
Prof. Hauhouot Asseypo (Côte d'Ivoire)

Like all regions, Africa must deal with the impact of the knowledge revolution, societal complexity and the reality of globalization. Since the Earth Summit (Rio, 1992), Africa has made insufficient progress towards the goal of sustainable development. Problems still unresovled include *environmental degradation, excessive urbanization, armed conflict and dangerous levels of illness and poverty.*

Concurrently, higher education is expected to help to find remedies. This will require much greater transdisciplinarily in programmes, modernized institutional structures and a clear commitment to lifelong learning for all citizens.

To compensate for limited funding, great hope is invested in international co-operation notably collaboration with NGOs and IGOs such as the African Association of Universities, AUPELF-UREF and UNESCO. Universities must pool resources and share knowledge across regions—perhaps this is the only really effective scenario for the future.

Co-operative action launched by CRUFAOCI (The Rectors' Conference of French-speaking Western Africa) includes the following fields: *geographical data systems in the Côte d'Ivoire, food production in Senegal, forestry in Gabon, the marine sciences in Madagascar.*

❑ Creating International Learning Environments
Prof. Dr. Rietje van Dam Mieras (The Netherlands)

Universities have to think critically about their local and global roles in society and reflect on the use of information and communication technology in knowledge transfer processes. Universities generate and transfer knowledge via education; they must also specialize in the integration of disciplines and transfer of knowledge to society at large. This task is much broader and requires more co-operative action. The new opportunities created in the rapidly developing field of information and communication technology are highly promising in this respect. They offer universities new possibilities to share knowledge and expertise and to change from 'knowledge islands' into nodes in a knowledge network. Each node has its own identity and characteristics, but draws knowledge and expertise from a much larger reservoir.

An example of a co-operative international learning environment is the Global Seminar on Environment,

Agriculture and Sustainable Development co-ordinated by Cornell University. Universities from the USA, Honduras, Costa Rica, Sweden and the Netherlands create together an international learning environment in which staff members and students with different cultural backgrounds work together. A rich blend of classical face-to-face teaching, computer conferencing, and videoconferencing is used. This is exciting, not because of the technology, but because of the social interaction and exchange of views between individuals with different cultural backgrounds.

The Global Seminar approach is only one example of the use of ICTs in a learning process. The addition of an international dimension to the learning environment is important but information and communication technology can be used in many different ways—in research and education and also to transfer knowledge to society in a broader sense. Information and communication technology becomes an instrument in creating a more sustainable future.

❑ Capacity Building: the Key to Sustainable Human Development
Dr. Kirit Parikh (UNDP)

Economic trends over the last several decades have changed our thinking about development. Today, it is generally recognized that:

- Development is more than economic growth and increase in income. A more holistic concept of human development is the objective. In addition to income growth, literacy, good health, ability to withstand unexpected events provided by own wealth, family support or social or public institutions, dignity and freedom are considered important elements of human well-being and of the notion of sustainable human development (SHD).
- Top-down approaches to development have had limited success in achieving holistic development.

A society committed to sustainable human development needs capacities at various levels: individual, institutional, social and governmental. The sum total of these capacities should create a society that effectively ensures wide participation in decision-making to address relevant concerns, that has the technical competence to identify options and select optimal policy from amongst them, that is able to efficiently execute the policy through appropriate governance and regulatory mechanisms, and that is adaptive in its policies and institutions. Thus, it remains relevant to changing contexts and circumstances by being receptive to feedback and by avoiding excessive bureaucracy.

Six kinds of capacities are needed:

- capacity for mobilizing effective participation in projects;
- capacities to function in a globalizing world with rapid technological change;
- capacity to manage transition to a market economy;
- capacity to benefit from FDIs (Foreign Direct Investment);
- capacity to manage technology;
- capacity to manage a freer economy.

❑ Sustainable Human Development and Students—Investing in the Future
Mr. Patrick Mpedzisi (Zimbabwe)

Students' participation in the curricula, in the recreational and even in the daily running of their institutions equips them with the necessary skills to tackle complex situations and problems. If students are integrated properly and democratically into institutional structures, they learn to respond in a democratic manner. Students should learn to live in a culture of peace, accepting other ethnic groups and races, communicating with different generations. For this, institutional structures play a facilitating role and can ensure efficient and reliable dissemination of information.

It is no enough for data on Sustainable Human Development (literature, knowledge and practice) to be concentrated in institutions alone. Individuals must personally adopt new ways of thinking and acting. Student participation at all institutional levels gives young people the voice to determine their future in a committed manner. This develops a sense of responsibility, which is the basis of personal and individual initiative. Student participation should also have a global dimension. This promotes a concerted effort from students worldwide, broadens perspectives and encourages collaboration in solving international dilemmas and global complexities. For this, the new information technologies are essential.

A society concerned about its future should begin by investing in those groups who will shape the future. In Higher Education institutions, this means the students. They are in positions where information is accessible to them and they also provide the link between today's stakesholders and tomorrow's decision-makers. Students are able to decipher the concise and elevated diction of the policymakers while understanding the enthusiastic and inexperienced views of young people. This continues the Sustainable Development ethic between the generations. So, investing in students is a sustainable activity.

Points to Further Reflection

- What specific issues would be addressed by a *University Platform for a Sustainable Future* in the socio-economic and cultural context of your country?
- What examples can be cited from your country with regard to innovative practice in *university management, curriculum development, professional training, research and knowledge transfer?*
- Could a national scheme be set up to aware prizes for innovative institutions and who might fund this?
- In relation to environmental conservation, could a similar award scheme be envisaged for model "Green Universities?"
- The Earth Summit (Rio de Janeiro 1992) adopted *Agenda* 21; Chapter 36 of this document deals with *Education, Public Awareness and Training*. How can

universities in your country contribute to a *"Local Agenda 21"* scheme (i.e. the contribution of universities to raising public awareness of environmental problems and their role in taking remedical action)?

- What advocacy role can national and regional university associations play in promoting the concept and practice of sustainable human development—both amongst their members and in relation to national decision-makers?

15

Contributing to National and Regional Development

Viewpoints: United Kingdom, Spain, Cameroon, Tunisia, Canada

Not only has regional or local intervention become more important to economic success, but there has been a qualitative shift in the form of local policy towards indigenous entrepreneurship and innovation, and to providing a more sophisticated environment for mobile capital so as to maximize local "value added" (e.g. R & D and other higher status jobs, successful and therefore growing firms). This leads to a greater concern to harness university education and research to specific economic and social objectives.

Nowhere is this demand for specificity more clear than in the field of regional development. While universities are located in regions, questions are being asked about what contribution they make to the development of those regions? Whilst it might be possible to identify passive impacts of universities in terms of direct and indirect employment, how can the resources of universities be mobilized to actively contribute to the development process?

This implies a better understanding of universities on the part of regional actors and agencies and of regional dynamics on the part of the universities. An obvious starting point for such an understanding can be provided by an audit of existing regionally relevant activities with the audit being jointly commissioned by universities and regional agencies. It may be that regional agencies have not clearly articulated regional needs and there may have been many missed opportunities for productive engagement. To reveal these opportunities, it will be necessary for universities to enter into a dialogue with various stakeholders in the regional development process (e.g. local and regional elected authorities, employers and employers' organizations, regional media).

Improved integration of universities with regional development will not be readily achieved by top down planning mechanisms at either the institutional or regional level but by ensuring that the various stakeholders in the regional development process—education and training providers, employers' organizations, trade unions, economic development and labour market agencies, and individual teachers and learners—have an understanding of one another's roles and the factors encouraging or inhibiting greater regional engagement.

The paper suggests that regional criteria could be incorporated into national teaching and research assessment exercises. These criteria include, inter alia, *regional engagement as part of the academic mainstream, mapping and measuring this engagement, collaboration, partnerships, human resource development, distinctive institutional focus, the geographical identity of the region, regional policy and leadership, communicating regional needs and priorities and reflecting these in the teaching and learning processes, anticipating future development, and institutional responsiveness to new challenges.*

Regional Viewpoints

❑ Regional Considerations in a Global World
Prof. Joseph Bricall (Spain)

Three factors merit attention in this debate:

- today, all development, including the regional, must take account of global trends. Every country is situating its social progress in relation to the globalization phenomenon, and this reality should also dominate regional planning. As no area or sub-entity can afford to be marginalized or isolated, this holds true for regional universities;

- over the past 20 years, there has been extraordinary growth in student numbers with many coming from new socio-economic and cultural groups. This democratization is positive and has necessitated new types of institutions with new missions—notably to meet the demand for employment-related skills. But, this demand is also global and so older universities should take stock of their role and impact in their specific communities;
- last but not least, the advent of the Learning Society has meant new forms of knowledge, delivered by new methods and for new publics who will use it in newly organized work environments. This has engendered a complex and ongoing debate on the links between universities and the world of work. Since society contributes much to these institutions, they, in turn, should take due note of demand and strive to satisfy this within their own particular community.

❑ Meeting National, Regional and International Needs
Prof. Dorothy Njeuma (Cameroon)

Cameroon is a country composed of regions (two English-speaking provinces and eight which are francophone) and with two systems of education and their examination structures running in parallel.

Since 1993, there have been six universities serving the specific needs of different areas. However, there is also reciprocity of enrolment and exchange of students, whatever their linguistic background. The University of Buea, located in an essentially rural area but one which has an important industrial presence, is a non-residential institution which has experienced exponential growth in recent years.

Because Cameroon's universities are state-owned and funded, regional bodies have a lesser role in their development.

Nevertheless, the impact of these institutions on their areas is very strong and the benefits for growth are clear. This is proven by the dynamic interaction between universities and local communities and industries.

However, each university must be able to act locally, nationally and globally. Today, this is the greatest challenge for African institutions which must strengthen their ICT capacities to deal with this task despite problems of access and infrastructure.

❑ Universities of the South as Agents of Development
Prof. Brahim Baccari (Tunisia)

Regional development should contribute to national development which is a crucial goal for developing nations where the university plays a key role in the identity of the country. Also, the South has much less experience of university partnerships with the economic sector but is now ready to respond to this call in the interests of social progress.

Certainly, the university, as well as industry and the business sector, must now be a motor of national development which means forging new relations with a variety of partners to meet social needs. This will necessitate the modernization of institutional structures, of curriculum and of teaching. Above all, young people must learn to manage the knowledge and know-how acquired through higher education so as to become real agents of development.

As society changes, so higher education must evolve to deal with new economic and technological challenges. Yet, universities must remain the guardians of national history and culture; as the conscience of a nation, they must not only create knowledge but participate in its application for development. Modern systems and institutions of higher education must balance this tension between analysis and active involvement in social problem-solving.

❑ Canada: A National of Regions
Prof. Susan Clark (Canada)

In a sense, all Canadian Universities are regional because they are funded by the 10 provinces and largely draw their student populations from these. The vast geographical and economic diversity of Canada serves to confirm this character. Moreover, a region has specific social, economic and cultural dimensions, as is witnessed by the role of Quebec.

Recent changes in the national economy from dependence on primary industry to more varied local economies has forced a reappraisal of higher education and the employability of graduates. As a result, institutions must operate in dual mode by combining teaching and research and by orienting themselves to both local and global conditions.

Despite present turbulence, the fundamental mission of the university remains valid i.e. to provide a sound basic education for good citizenship. Governments must be encouraged to promote this mission and to balance public and private support to higher education institutions.

Finally, governments and the public at large must know what these institutions really do. When this is the case, their accountability is greatly facilitated.

Points for Further Reflection

- How can interaction be fostered among knowledge producers, disseminators and users so as to lead to the collective representation of interests and a mutual awareness of a common purpose?
- Could it be interesting to carry out audits to identity "appropriate skills" for university graduates (to depend on the region's overall development strategy) and the university's contribution to social and community development?
- The rapidly changing needs of employers and the labour market affect curriculum. Universities have been good at the *know-what* and *know-why* aspects of education and are improving on the *know-how* aspects through incorporation of the tacit learning acquired via work placements into teaching programmes. However, the *know-who* dimension is altogether more problematic. How can this be tackled?

- Could international networks play a role in the reduction of uncertainties and the sharing of knowledge?
- Could regional criteria be incorporated into national teaching and research assessment exercises?
- Could more fundamental training and support be provided for those acting as the link between different organizations (e.g. for skills such as networking, facilitation, working with alternative cultures, setting up projects, planning and contract management, raising financial support)?
- What are the consequences of university-region interaction within your university?

16

Higher Education Staff Development

Viewpoints: Malaysia, Germany, Egypt, International Federation of University Women (IFUW), Association of African Universities (AAU).

Staff development is central to the quality of higher education. The emerging trend towards greater institutional autonomy has led to a new focus on what leaders, managers and academics should be doing.

New Expectations for Tertiary Institutions

Today, institutions must: handle increasing numbers of part-time and mature students (meaning longer staff hours), serve regional needs via links to associated providers, offer the same material via dual mode tuition and with the same staff, equip students with general transferable skills to meet employers' needs, stimulate faculty to reach out to community priorities, offer research and consultancy services to local industry and commerce.

Challenges for Institutional Leaders

- providing strategic guidance and an institutional vision;
- obtaining resources from business, donors and alumni to replace government's find;
- encouraging an innovative, entrepreneurial culture supported by institutional processes;

- pursuing institutional goals in a community which is instinctively suspicious of such things.

Competencies for Institutional Managers

- people management skills, such as team building and helping staff to develop themselves academically and professionally;
- numeracy and understanding of financial and cost issues;
- IT awareness;
- sensitivity to new developments in the external environment, such as competitive threats;
- customer consciousness;
- strategic awareness of the institutions' position;
- understanding of how to use institutional decision-making processes in a collegial environment.

Academic Staff Require

- awareness and understanding of the different ways in which students learn;
- knowledge, skills and attitudes to assess the student learning process;
- commitment to scholarship, professional standards and knowledge of current developments;
- awareness of IT applications to the discipline (for materials and teaching);
- sensitivity to external "market" signals regarding employers' needs;
- mastery of new pedagogical developments including "dual mode" tuition challenges;
- customer awareness, as regards the views and aspirations of stakeholders, including students;
- understanding of the impact of international/multi-cultural factors on the curricula;

- teaching students with different profiles (age, backgrounds, race) throughout a longer day;
- skills to handle large student numbers in lectures, seminars or workshops without losing quality;
- development of personal and professional "coping strategies".

Skills for Researchers

- proposal writing; networking and fund raising for projects; managing Ph.D. students and researchers; project management, particularly relating to international partnership projects.

Administrative Staff now face the following environment

Administrative staff must have solid Information Technology skills, be genuinely aware of costs, sensitive to a wide range of student needs and adapt to flexible work practices as cost-cutting continues.

Worldwide these challenges will vary according to the scale and capacities of institutions. However, overall, three strategies will be essential:

- a sound policy for initial and ongoing training for institutional staff at all levels;
- attractive working conditions and incentives schemes for staff motivation;
- enhanced international co-operation in the areas of staff development to share good practice.

Regional Viewpoints

❑ Staff Development: Issues Facing Developing Countries
Dr. Jasbir Singh (Malaysia)

Staffing Problems

The need to upgrade staff qualifications remains the top priority. Data assembled in 1990 suggested that recruitment could not keep pace with student expansion. The rapid growth since 1990 in the developing countries has placed further pressure on recruitment of appropriate persons. The post-graduate sector remains small, relatively, to provide a competitive base for recruitment. Considerable numbers are still recruited with a first or masters' degree. In 1991, most developing countries staff with doctoral degrees ranged from 40 to about 10% compared with 50-60% in developed countries. Recent data suggests that the situation has improved marginally but not significantly. In some countries there still remains the added dimension of needing local staff to replace expatriate staff. Poor remuneration has been identified as the principal cause of attrition among senior academic staff, leading to a steady loss of university staff to non-university employment. Pursuit of other income-generating activities has also resulted in poor teaching, minimal participation in university administration and policy making and a neglect of research.

Professional Development ot Staff

Delivery mechanisms need to be both efficient and cost-effective for developing countries. A number of models are:

- India has 45 Academic Staff Colleges funded by the University Grants Commission. Their aim is to upgrade knowledge and skills through Orientation Programmes and Refresher Courses. These are supplemented by specialist refresher courses in selected Indian universities and by courses organized at the initiative of teachers, colleges, universities and institutions.
- Some countries benefit from a regional network for staff development such as the University Staff Development in Eastern and Southern Africa network (USDESA) established at the University of Zimbabwe in 1991 to promote activities in he sub-region.
- In the United Kingdom, the Universities' Staff Development Unit (USDU) at Sheffield University oversees a range of nationally provided courses. An Institute of Teaching and Learning has been proposed by the Dearing Report.

- Some developing countries have a national centre to co-ordinate all staff development activities.
- Elsewhere, institutions are establishing staff development units to train and support their own staff.

❑ Europe: The Increasing Relevance of Academic Staff Development Programmes
Dr. Brigitte Berendt (Germany)

Western Europe

- *Great Britain:* In 1997, 125 higher education institutions had staff development units.
- *The Netherlands:* In 1996, 11 out of 13 universities offered staff development programmes.
- *France:* A national plan provides "practice-orientated pedagogical training", performed by 14 academic staff development units, or the national association ADMES.
- *Germany:* Since 1993, applicants for a professorship have to give evidence of their pedagogical skills (e.g. by participation in academic staff development courses). Today, excellence in teaching is as important as excellence in research.
- *Switzerland:* In 1996, universities offered programmes including up to 15 workshops per semester.
- *Austria:* In 1998, all teaching staff members of polytechnics had to attend courses.
- *Finland.* All universities offer courses. A national staff development unit is being discussed.
- *Norway:* A national committee for staff development co-ordinates courses.
- *Spain* and *Ireland:* Different universities offer promising programmes.

Eastern Europe

Eastern European universities often regard academic staff development programmes carried out in Western European countries as an important tool to "democratize" universities and the society. But many of them face other priorities, and necessary funds are not available. There are, however, promising efforts in, inter alia, *Slovenia, Czech Republic, Slovakia and Belarus.*

❑ Co-operation Strategies in Staff Development
Prof. Dr. Abdel-Karim Aboul-Hassan-Arab Network on Staff Development (Egypt)

Networks of Centres of Excellence in the South

These centres can strengthen higher education in the developing world provided they are:

- well identified (e.g. The Third World Academy of Sciences);
- linked thematically and equipped with ICTs;
- offering graduate and postgraduate training with scholarship support;
- networked to their counterparts in the North.

Regional Foundations for Higher Education

These should be joint donor initiatives. Most needed is a foundation for Africa with a capital fund of about US$ 1 million. Its investment income could:

- improve institutional research and training infrastructure;
- provide postgraduate fellowships at Centres of Excellence in the South;
- attract regional experts thereby stemming the Brain Drain;
- bring Northern experts to help capacity-building.

❑ Higher Education Staff Development: Where are the Women Leaders?
Dr. E.M.E. Poskitt—International Federation of University Women (IFUW)

The Problem

In virtually no field and no country are women the majority of leadership positions in universities. Women are around 10%

of Professors, 34% of Lecturers; rarely Vice-Chancellors or Deans but more commonly Registrars and Chief Librarians. The enormous gain to a country of women with higher education in the workforce should be acknowledged and made visible.

What is to be done?

1. ensure enforcement of Equal Opportunities legislation;
2. educate all grades of staff and students of the advantages and importance of reaching equitable distribution of women throughout the workforce;
3. make staff and students aware of gender issues in curricula and training and implement policies which encourage gender equality throughout the institution;
4. develop, maintain and use gender disaggregated statistical records for applications, admissions, appointments, achievements, etc.;
5. review job descriptions, career environment and opportunities for staff development and training, so as to create more humane structures within higher education institutions;
6. develop family friendly policies within higher education institutions: flexible hours: crèches, allowances for maternity leave for graduate students, etc.;
7. study the potential for a "woman friendly university" in each higher education institution: This can be described as "a place where every woman feels comfortable living, studying, working and playing—a place where she can reach her full academic and personal potential."

❑ Staff Development—Two African Priorities
Prof. Narciso Matos—Association of African Universities (AAU)

Staff Development and Information and Communication Systems

New Information and Communication Technologies are vital for academic activity. Developing countries and African universities must be connected electronically to benefit from information which is otherwise not available.

But ICT use in university administration, libraries, and management information systems, is very limited. This isolates staff from international networks and limits their participation in the world pool of knowledge and information. It also narrows the possibilities for staff training and attractive conditions of work.

Regional Co-operation in Staff Development

The AAU has over the years promoted the Study Programme on Higher Education Management and Research in Africa, and the Management Training Workshops (SUMA Workshops) for senior university leaders. These programmes addressing university financing, cost sharing, strategic planning and gender equity, represent regional approaches to staff development and its application to academic management.

These programmes should be extended to deans, heads of departments, librarians and other university administrators. They also reveal the need to establish continued programmes instead of sporadic mid one-off types of training opportunities. The case can be made for an African institute to train and provide academic leaders with modern management and leadership skills.

Points for Further Reflection

- How can one encourage staff within institutions to push for staff development to be provided?
- Are trade union bodies helping to facilitate more staff development initiatives? Can this be enhanced by national or international supports networks?
- How much should institutions invest in staff development? How can proper priority and fund finding for this be assured?
- What else should institutions do to promote effective staff development activities?

- How can institutional leaders promote a culture where staff development is seen as essential and is welcomed?
- Can distance learning solutions help staff development needs?
- How can national buffer bodies or governments help in this area?
- How best can international bodies and agencies help countries with small or under-resourced higher education systems?
- Can staff development networks operate effectively via member subscriptions without external funding or will they always need support?
- Given the core competencies needed by a member of teaching staff, how much specialization should be encouraged?
- How can staff, themselves, push for staff development services?

17

Higher Education and Society:
A Student Perspective

Viewpoints: United Kingdom, Republic of the Congo, Indonesia, Denmark, Egypt, Brazil, Turkey, Cuba, Palestine, Ghana, Nepal, the People's Republic of China, and United States of America, Malta, Kenya, Iran, France, Colombia, Germany, South Africa and the world of work.

This debate examined the issues and concerns of students at the higher education level on the eve of the 21st century. This followed on from a request in 1995 by the Director-General of UNESCO as part of the 50th anniversary of the Organization, to solicit the student perspective on the process of change now underway in this sector on a global scale.

Traditionally, higher education has provided the wisdom and expertise which equip young people for their future roles as social leaders. This must and will remain a fundamental task for higher education since this sector has promoted the values and attitudes which are those of socially responsible citizens.

Today, the role and profile of students in higher education has become extremely varied. In response to the reality of the mass demand, the necessity to diversify has become a challenge for every country. Issues such as access, quality, relevance and internationalization are under closer scrutiny and students are insisting on greater dialogue between the partners involved so that they may select courses which permit them to accede to acceptable levels of employment, hence to social development.

This debate then aimed to legitimize the student voice in the discussions amongst stakeholders in the higher education sector. While this situation may exist already in many countries, it is by no means universal. UNESCO thus considered that this recognition of the student perspective was essential in order to ensure that the debate on the reform and renewal of higher education included the views of the principal beneficiaries.

Remarks of the Chairperson—Baroness Tessa Blackstone (United Kingdom)

Broader access witnesses to the democratization of higher education and to the recognition of the rights of citizens. Consequently, it must be a priority for the specific development agenda of each and every nation. However, high quality higher education is an expensive undertaking for governments which are faced with many pressing problems. Today, they need convincing evidence that their investment in the sector is justified and so higher education institutions must respond with imagination and innovative practices. Today, there is vast experimentation where all countries, both regionally and internationally, have much to learn from one another in tackling fundamental areas such as degree structure, the renewal of the curriculum and of teaching and learning methods.

Remarks of Federico Mayor (Director-General of UNESCO, 1987-1999)

Social exclusion is the gravest problem faced by the world today. As the Third Millennium will be the age of information, of knowledge and of sophisticated technological expertise, education has become the sole means of rendering these vital commodities available to all citizens. In this regard, higher education must change so as to become the principal vehicle of lifelong learning and so to realize people's aspirations for education and, so, for social advancement.

Higher education is an ongoing "rebellion without violence" which reaffirms its classic and legitimate role as critic of society.

Society and Higher Education Systems of Quality and Relevance

- Views from the Republic of the Congo, Indonesia, Denmark, Egypt and Brazil

Higher education has a crucial social responsibility in the promotion of sustainable human development, in the defence of human rights, in the construction of democracy in all countries and in the promotion of the values and knowledge which ensure social integration. One of its primary tasks should be to prepare students for roles of social, political and cultural leadership.

Access to higher education must be equitable for all citizens, based on the principle of merit and regardless of gender, religion, ethnic or socio-economic background. In this regard, the use of Information and Communication Technologies (ICTs) has an important democratic function.

Students insist on their recognition as full partners in higher education. They are not merely "clients" which is, to them, a limited definition. Rather they wish to be full parties in discussions related to decision-making. In this regard, freedom of expression, co-operation and dialogue amongst all stakeholders is seen as the way forward to promoting responsible citizenship.

To this end, it is essential to widen the scope of their participation in policy and decision-making at all levels—institutional, national, regional and international. Areas such as curricula reform and evaluation would benefit as a result.

Global problems require humanistic solutions from people who possess the capacity to interact with partners form other cultural backgrounds.

Parado xically, students must face the reality of current socio-economic climate where, often, educational policies are based on market-oriented approaches and thus do not have the resources required to build capacities with long-term impact.

Regional Perspectives on Higher Education

- Views from Turkey, Cuba, Palestine, Ghana, Nepal, the People's Republic of China and the United States

Higher education institutions must be amongst the principal actors in the process of social change. Their role is, on one hand, to produce new knowledge in concert with a variety of other partners; and on the other hand, to help shape the complex reality of social transformation. They should enable the leaders of tomorrow to promote and uphold a culture of peace in all societies. In this pursuit, they should receive appropriate government support.

Different societies clearly require different models of higher education. A single model of higher education and especially a model which may emphasize privatization would contradict the right of all to education. To avoid this outcome, adequate funding support for students, in the form of scholarships and grants, is essential.

Adequate funding also depends on the fairness of structural adjustment programmes whose harsh conditions can prevent countries from meeting their obligations to their student populations.

Dialogue amongst students, national and institutional decision-makers and the professoriate is still far from the norm in a number of regions.

The growth i- demand has put new light on the role and responsibility of students. Choices should be more student-led and make adequate provision for life-long learning. Student NGOs have much to contribute in this instance.

Mobility—whether physical or intellectual—promotes the sharing of knowledge and experience and acts as a tool to promote multicultural understanding and academic freedom. However, the funding for mobility schemes must be strengthened to ensure greater equity in North/South and East/West exchange patterns.

Many instances of conflict-ridden societies can be found across all regions and even in the industrialized countries. The culture of peace is thus an important priority to foster sound socio-economic and cultural development.

Social exclusion remains a reality of higher education in all regions. This may involve, inter alia, handicapped students, graduate students obliged to work and research at the same time or professors with long-term unstable working conditions. Such anomalies must be corrected as a matter of equity in higher education.

Producing Entrepreneurial Graduates

- Views from Malta, Kenya, Iran, France, Colombia, Germany, South Africa and the world of work

The profound changes in the nature of work—the volatility and rapid changes in the labour market—mean that graduate profiles must change. Aspects such as lifelong learning and the international validation of degrees have assumed crucial importance in the management and planning of higher education. Acquisition of essential entrepreneurial skills required for one's working life can now be the legitimate expectation of each graduate. These should be part and parcel of the modernization process of the curriculum and of pedagogical methods.

Entrepreneurship is a question of attitude—it denotes graduates with imagination, will, readiness to experiment, resilience, flexibility, broad understanding of socio-cultural and economic parameters, and flair in contrast to sheer academic brilliance. Graduates can now be of any age and profile—hence, it must be admitted that entrepreneurial skills can be acquired at any point of the learning process.

Consequently, traditional capacities such as analytical and research competencies must be complemented by social, communication and inter-personal skills. This is a tall order when dealing with massified higher education enrolments and doubly difficult for developing countries with insufficient institutional infrastructure. Moreover, a new profile of professor will also be needed—namely, one who understands the demands of the world of work.

The need to acquire such skills is largely due to the arrival of globalization which should be recognized as a social as well as an economic phenomenon. As a result, all regions require graduates with broad understanding of our multicultural world and who possess the necessary flexibility to adapt to rapid change, Proactive experiences are considered vital to assure this acquisition: for example, working in groups and communities such as NGOs, undertaking internships in the professional sector, and initiating individual co-operation projects.

The building of partnerships will be a crucial factor in promoting new graduate profiles. At the present time, distrust exists amongst certain areas of society but this must be eliminated if constructive alliances are to be forged.

This interaction must be a bottom-up process starting with students themselves and fully supported by higher education institutions, by students and by employers. Their co-operation should be based on shared ethical values so as to lay the necessary foundation for effective interface.

Points for Further Reflection

Advocacy

How can advocacy skills be better acquired?

(NB: These skills refer to understanding and defending student interests in relation to institutional governance/ management, teaching and learning degree recognition, legal instruments covering student rights, interface with the community and with employers).

What strategies can strengthen the student presence in national, institutional, economic and community decision-making bodies?

How can student NGOs best fulfil their mission in this regard at national, regional and international level?

Training

How can training opportunities (in social leadership and in professional fields) be increased?

How can training in advocacy for student interests be ensured?

Research

How can student-related research be promoted to:

- know more about their status and conditions in different contexts/
- ensure regular monitoring of their needs in relation to their professional development?
- involve all relevant stakesholders in this investigative exercise?

Goals for 2010

How can the following goals be achieved in different countries?

- presence of the student voice in every national decision-making body for higher education
- a 30% increase (where required) in the access to higher education of the 18-24 age crop cohort
- establishment or extension, in every country, of a national mechanism to permit dialogue between students and the employment sector
- establishment, through international support, of appropriate legal instruments which aim to protect the rights and conditions of students.

18

New Information Technologies

Viewpoints: Mexico, France, Canada, Hungary, United States of America, Denmark

Most technical and methodological solutions necessary to develop the New Information and Communication Technologies, such as the Internet, originate in the scientific community. Paradoxically, the education sector is the field which has benefited least from what NICTs have brought. And, the present information environment is characterized by the mass advent of digital solutions which are drastically changing established realities. Universities must now reflect on these uses and their impact on education and research.

Some consider that 'the industrialization of education' has arrived. Are buildings, lecture rooms and auditoriums liable to be replaced by digital sites and virtual seats of learning? Will teachers be replaced by digital avatars? Will they have the ability to redefine their roles, or will they be subjected to the changes imposed by globalization?

The NICTs are revolutionizing open and distance education and should enable it to emerge from the scepticism of educationists to become a global industry. The concepts of 'collaboration' and 'asynchronous education' should gradually become established because they reflect the necessity of solid change. This change foretells a veritable educational revolution, in which the traditional space-time-hierarchy structures will be shattered.

The concept of the virtual university helps to meet the future challenges of academics. It presupposes that the NICTs will be used and that the various technological tools will be combined 'in proportion' with a view to radically altering the cost of education. The educational methods accompanying the new technological paradigm promote a participatory vision of education via asynchronous learning, a new inter-actor relationship and 'lifelong' education.

The virtual university may be regarded as a 'meta-university' which provides support for existing universities, particularly those of the South, through distance education infrastructure, advice and assistance in the creation of the necessary structures, shared educational material, technical and human resources to facilitate the preparation of on-line educational material.

The mass advent of the NICTs in the years ahead raises the question of how the teaching profession can prepare for these changes. 'New teachers' must master this new NICT environment and be mentally prepared for a new role while still expanding their knowledge of their subject.

Information is becoming globalized into a 'market'. And the need is growing for free access to information in the form of a universal public service for the research and education sector.

The introduction of ICTs in higher education does, however, present certain dangers. The economic imbalance between North and South penalizes the latter. The scientific excellence of the industrialized countries must reach the poorest countries for co-development. As the risk of 'infopoverty' curbs development, universities should be a main source of the circulation of knowledge in the service of shared collective intelligence.

Regional Viewpoints

- The Information Culture ... And beyond
  Prof. Lourdes Feria (Mexico)

In the academic environment, the *Information Culture* depends on the excellence of four components: *technological infrastructure, professorial capacity in this field, multimedia materials and strong electronic library and information services.*

This means that the actual process of being informed—including the development of good critical capacities—is more vital than the information instruments themselves. The Information Culture has two objectives: to encourage students *to learn how to learn* and to ensure the continuation of this attitude *beyond the lecture hall into their careers and throughout life.* Each student should understand the role of information, use this correctly and assess its value.

The virtual university has great access potential and could lead from information to knowledge for learners—provided that individual reflection and intellectual contribution are safeguarded. The ultimate result will be improved competitiveness, since methods require learners to be innovative, creative and to think critically. From learning how to learn, they learn how to be entrepreneurial.

However, the final goal of this Information Culture must be a better society with greater equality of opportunity based on mutual respect amongst all peoples.

❑ The Distance University as a Public Service
Prof. Bernard Loing (France)

A public service can be defined as an essential good to be available as of right to the entire community—free of charge or at low cost.

Opening access to higher education and the extensive use of technology have transformed the university into a sort of model of universal public service—e.g. *the British Open University, Portugal's Aberta University and the Fern Universität in Germany*. These have a dual character:

- a national mandate since they are created for all citizens and largely funded by the State;
- a social function as they are intended to reduce inequalities by opening university courses to disadvantaged, handicapped and minority students.

Being universities at the national level, these establishments have often played a major role in the overall development of higher education (e.g. Turkey, Thailand, India, China).

Though previously hostile to this mode, traditional universities are now copying this model with distance learning departments, expanding websides and courses taught by virtual methods. So, Communication Technology helps to meet the educational needs of a changing world where:

- *ongoing training is vital since knowledge is quickly obsolete*
- *lifelong learning has become the norm*
- *the labour market is uncertain*
- *new professions with new profiles have emerged*
- *training must be adapted to constraints of time and place*
- *individual and self-taught learning situations are common.*

Thus, higher distance learning offers a public service to the greatest number of people.

❑ Virtual University Networks—The French Canadian Case Prof. Dyane Adam (Canada)

Based on the experience of a consortium of French-speaking Canadian universities, six aspects of the Virtual University merit attention:

- The **technological infrastructure** permits teaching via multimedia (e.g. video and audio conferencing, INTERNET, computer areas). Agreement must be reached on the compatibility of equipment, purchasing contracts, maintenance, pooling resources and joint requests for government support.
- **Governance and consultation procedures** necessitate inter-institutional planning at various levels: rectors, managers, timetabling, editorial

committees and protocols regarding student mobility and credit transfer.

- **Course programming** determines how qualifications are delivered e.g. those taught entirely by distance methods *(the Ottawa University B. Ed. at Glendon University College)* or those jointly taught and accredited *(the Masters in Orthophonics from Laurentian and Ottawa).*
- **Multimedia course material and teaching tools** are developed jointly in digital or printed forms *(e.g. an INTERNET course in Psychology, a CD Rom on French minorities and the Biodidac webites-www.biodidac.uottawa.ca, website bibliopol).*
- **Pedagogical training** for teachers is jointly provided via NICTs, teaching guides and group discussion on technology usage.
- **Online networks of researchers** are established.

❑ Integrating Technology into University Life
Prof. Tamás Lajos (Hungary)

Three levels of application of ICT can be identified.

In the first "low profile" approach, individual lectures use *technology for enhancing the effectiveness of their teaching.* Communication with students via E-mail, using Internet for making course materials and literature available are typical applications.

The second "higher profile" approach is the *systematic integration of technology in the life—not only in the education—of the institution.* This needs considerable investment and operational costs. A top down approach, strong technical support, standardization, extensive staff development, and structured teamwork characterize this method. Such features are a departure from traditional academic activities, which are based on individual initiatives and achievements, integrated research and education, and academic freedom.

The third "high profile" approach is *the implementation of the virtual university concept.* Because of the fundamental change involved, large scale investments are needed along with deep transformation of university structures, culture and even mission. Establishing relevant new units and co-operating with outside institutions can help manage change.

❑ Managing Open Learning Systems
Prof. Michel Moreau (France)

The innovative potential of open and virtual learning systems greatly depends on the efficient management of three complementary functions:

- *The organization of training and personalized services; in this regard, logistics must be excellent including the overall planning process which is vital when numbers are large.*
- *The training of the staff involved; here, much can be learned from successful practice. Open learning ultimately depends on the quality of the teaching staff-though they may not always be in universities.*
- *The production of materials, notably those using multimedia techniques. This aspect needs team work and an experimental approach. Cultural specificity must be respected, despite the temptation to cater for the mass market.*

Today, many governments wish to develop their higher learning systems and take advantage of the huge international demand for training. But developing countries must identify the most relevant teaching approaches and the best pedagogical use of new technologies has yet to be realized. The developing world must insist on these important dimensions.

❑ The UCAID Project: Realizing the Potential of ICTs
Prof. Molly Corbett Broad (U.S.A.)

The extend the promise of ICTs for higher education, over 130 leading American universities have joined government and industrial partners to establish the *University Corporation for Advanced Internet Development* (*UCAID*). This provides direction for creating cutting-edge computing and telecommunication network capabilities required by the academic community. A major UCADID project has been *Internet2*, focused on the development of new advanced networking applications needed by the higher education community:

1. ***Creating and sustaining a leading-edge network capacity for the United States' research and education community.*** In partnership with major ICT companies, UCAID initiated the Abilene Project to provide member universities with the advanced high-availability backbone network, necessary for supporting their advanced research applications, as well as a separate network capability for conducting research into the next generation of network design. Abilene's high-speed, high-handwidth network aims at supporting the network applications development efforts of Internet2.
2. ***Directing network development efforts to enable a generation of applications to exploit fully the capabilities of broadband networks*** (such as Abilene). Potential applications include media integration and Internet broadcast, real-time collaboration, and shared virtual reality environments. Such technologies are critical for research and scholarship, distance education and lifelong learning.
3. ***Integrating the work of Internet2 with ongoing efforts to improve general Internet services for the entire academic community and the global Internet.*** With corporate partners, UCAID will ensure the rapid transfer of the new network services and applications resulting from Internet2 and Abilene, to all levels of education and the broader Internet, both in the USA and internationally.

❑ Real Universities—The Knowledge Base
Prof. Henrik Toft Jensen (Denmark)

Institutions must ensure that normal student/professor contact will be a reality in the future.

Certainly, the function of the teacher must change from a "source of information" to a "source of knowledge and understanding" so as to educate and provide possibilities for learning. But education is much more than classroom activity. Campus and student activities remain important opportunities to develop both awareness and understanding.

Real universities and similar institutions must remain the core of higher education. But they have to be innovative and devise strategies for using ICTs in teaching, research, administration and libraries. For example, they could offer part of their teaching activities via Open and Distance Learning—the virtual part of the university.

Such delivery is important for special groups, such as those in lifelong learning who are restricted by time and space factors. Also, ICTs serve those parts of the world where there are few higher education institutions, where these are weak, or where population is scattered. This could help limit the brain drain. But virtual activities can never replace **real** institutions which develop—rather than merely transmit—knowledge. So, the main track is **the real** and the important side track is **the virtual.**

Universities must develop their ICT strategy in relation to cost. Information technology is big business and extremely expensive because it is quickly outdated. Governments should always evaluate ICT expenditure in terms of its contribution to strengthening the capacities of real institutions of higher education.

Points for Further Reflection

The new technological paradigm will lead to:

- *asynchronous learning*
- *a new inter-actor relationship*
- *lifelong learning*
- *a participatory vision of the educational process.*

In a particular social context:

- Is national and/or institutional policy with regard to NICT usage clearly developed and strategized?

- Are teachers and professors—i.e. the main agents—adequately trained to transmit skills in this area?
- Are appropriate 'template' software tools and strong logistic infastructures available to the academic community for the transmission of knowledge?
- Is sufficient research in progress with regard to the needs and impact of the new technological paradigm in education?
- How can NICT usage and virtual learning approaches take proper account of the following aspects: *regional diversity, co-development, scientific, excellence, intellectual property, the portability of teaching materials, quality assurance?*

19

Higher Education and Research

Viewpoints: International Council of Scientific Unions (ICSU), Italy, Senegal, India, Society for Research into Higher Education (SRHE), United States of America

Inspired by Cicero's statement that "only man possesses the capacity to seek and pursue truth," the 19th century scholar, Cardinal Newman defined the function of the ideal university as the pursuit of knowledge for its own sake.

Today, the university extends its functions to include the use of acquired knowledge to enhance—directly or indirectly—the material well-being, happiness and comfort of humankind. Higher education not only develops knowledge and trains young minds, but disseminates and applies such knowledge as well.

The 20th century will be remembered for its intellectual discoveries of relativity and quantum mechanics, and for the interpretation of the structure of DNA—discoveries that have enabled researchers to unravel some of nature's secrets and the fundamental behaviour of some of its life forms. The university's utilitarian perception of its mission, now regarded with greater emphasis and urgency, has largely resulted from these breakthroughs of knowledge in the natural sciences. Among their consequences are the fantastic development of information technology and high-tech industries, the increase in life-expectancy (chiefly because of advances in medical research and nutritional science), and increased food security (derived from genetic engineering research). In all these, the university has provided much of the leadership in partnership with government, industry and international agencies either as research collaborators or as funding bodies.

It is such achievements that have led to a revision of Newman's dictum. Of course there will continue to be programmes of liberal education devoted entirely to scholarly study of the major works of other scholars to help clarify and possibly modify one's previously held convictions. Pure scholarship will remain with us because of the persistence of the cherished value of freedom of thought and enquiry, that intellectual value upon which the life of the university as a place of research and teaching depends. But in recent times, the immense contributions that university research has made to the national economy ironically places in jeopardy the future funding of such work. The university itself appears to be moving away from its ancient tradition precisely because of the pressures of underfunding.

The new era will bring more problems but also challenges and opportunities. We need to ask what sort of human society we want to build in the next century; it must surely be one dominated by science and technology, but which engages all researchers. The words of Einstein should guide us in the next millennium.

"Concern for man himself and his fate must always form the chief interest of all technical endeavours; concern for the great unsolved problems of the organization of labour and the distribution of goods in order that the creations of our minds shall be a blessing and not a curse to mankind. Never forget this in the midst of your diagrams and equations."

❑ University—Industry Co-operation in Science and Technology
Prof. Albert E. Fischli—International Council of Scientific Unions (ICSU)

Fundamental or basic research is driven by the passion to understand—so, it has to remain flexible and open. Without new knowledge there can be no novel products or services.

Both universities and industry have an interest in collaborations. For universities, the driving forces are:

- market awareness of their own research projects;
- initiating, sustaining or enhancing research programmes;
- accessing private funding, on top of public financing;
- accessing complementary skills and facilities in industry;
- offering employment opportunities for research graduates.

For companies, the motivations are:

- outsourcing the R&D portfolio, especially at the discovery end;
- accessing complementary skills and facilities;
- gatekeeping emerging fields of science;
- developing global approaches to their own R&D;
- recruitment of research and technical staff.

Collaboration is based on agreements. The terms of the contacts have to be consistent with local competition laws and one main function should be to safeguard the intellectual property rights of investors.

Finally, collaboration between the academic creators of new knowledge and those who transform this into products and/or services in industry can be made successful by sound management, ongoing communication, the diversity of input and mutual benefits.

❑ Strengthening Essential Research Capacities in the South
Prof. Dr. Mohamed H.A. Hassan—The Third World Academy of Sciences (Italy)

Experience has shown that no country can achieve sustainable economic and social development without the support of a minimum core of indigenous, highly skilled and innovative scientists, technologists and other professionals, who can undertake basic and applied research essential to national development. In the majority of developing countries, especially the Least Developed Countries (LDCs), there is an acute shortage of world-class professionals. This is largely due to the failure of the institutions of higher education to attract, properly train and retain these professionals. The reasons are mainly attributed to the deteriorating infrastructure in universities and the acute shortage of leadership due to declining budgets and the brain drain. In addition, there has been a substantial increase in the student body, resulting in the over-production of poorly qualified graduates.

Basic sciences are the worst hit by this crisis. TWAS and ISP have conducted a survey on the status of Physics, Chemistry, Mathematics and Biology in Eastern and Southern Africa. It seems that the majority of countries in the region have an average of 5-8 Ph.D. holders in any of the four fields of Basic Sciences.

The challenge is to reverse this situation and create opportunities to attract and train young talents and sustain them to conduct problem-solving research. Networks of Centres of Excellence in the South and Regional Foundations to fund research would help nurture the capacities required.

In many developing countries, there is a strong political will to change and invest more in education and research but they are crippled by debt and globalization problems.

❑ Imperative for Improving North-South Co-operation in Research.
Prof. Oumar Sock (Senegal)

The potential of North/South and South/South co-operation depends on:

- a significant increase in resources, notably financial;
- the development of quality teaching and research in the South itself;
- enhanced academic mobility;
- stronger South/South co-operation backed up by institutions from the North;

- consolidation of existing research networks to share knowledge and know-how;
- much greater ICT capacities for the countries of the South which must acquire the necessary infrastructures, equipment and competencies to ensure that Information and Communication Technology is properly used. For instance, maintenance and renewal of equipment, control over the uses of ICTs and in their management are all essential.

Because these competencies are seriously lacking in the South, the gap with the North is widening very quickly. Marginalization is now a real threat in a world where the production and mastery of knowledge are the keys to development and social stability. This is the greatest danger: namely, that powerful ICTs are not controlled by a minority whose interests are served exclusively.

❑ Science as Human Creativity
Prof. M.G.K. Menon (India)

As we move into a future of multicultural diversity, we must make full use of distance learning and of continuing and interdisciplinary education, utilizing the powerful new tools provided by science and technology, but not necessarily keeping traditional institutional frameworks.

One crucial aspect is to increase public awareness of science as an intelligible, exciting and relevant domain.

Science and technology manifest the brilliance of human creativity, as well as its profound implications for society. This search for truth and for an understanding of nature and of the huge knowledge edifice which exists today are an intrinsic part of Culture. Though different in philosophy and method from Culture in the artistic sense, this still must derive from the multicultural character of our global village which makes human society so productive and interesting.

❑ Universal Networks: Accessing University Teaching and Research
Dr. Heather Eggins—Society for Research into Higher Education (United Kingdom)

The World Bank estimates that by 2025 perhaps 150 million individuals will seek higher education—often in low-income countries with inadequate infrastructure. Innovative course delivery will be needed. Some examples are:

- Open Learning Australia acts as a broker to make courses from Australian Universities available to students but does not, itself, grant degrees.
- The University of Maryland's university College teaches 55,000 students worldwide with degree ceremonies in Maryland, Heidelberg, Tokyo, Okinawa, Seoul, Schwabisch Gmund, Irkutsk and Vladivostok.
- The UK's Open University established in 1971 has registered some 2.5 million students, with 168,000 current students. It offers courses in Europe, including Eastern Europe, the Far East and has partnerships with American universities.
- The Western Governors' University whose founders include 17 governors and 14 business partners. Among these are IBM, Sun, AT&T, KPMG, Cisco, 3COM, Microsoft and International Thomson.
- The University of Phoenix, with 48,000 degree-credit students at 57 learning centres in 12 states, offers an on-line campus and specializes in particular areas at the BA completion and master's degree levels, especially in business, IT and teacher education.
- The DeVry Institute of Technology (in Chicago) enrols 48,000 students in business and technical programmes on 15 campuses in the USA and Canada. Other businesses proliferate such as Sylvan Learning Systems and, with MCI, the Caliber Learning Network.

The Internet offers indexing services for inquiries, CASO's Internet University holds information on 2,440 courses, the Global Network Academy lists 10,000 on-line courses.

A new industry is developing to help those who deliver courses via technology. World Space (Washington DC) is creating a global satellite-digital radio network, which will help Third World students. IBM Global Campus offers for sale a range of products including Lotus Notes and Learning Space which are tailored to the needs of distance learning. Convene International (San Francisco) and Microsoft have developed an Exchange Server-based distance learning system for universities.

❑ The Influence of the Media on Research
Prof. Maxwell McCombs (U.S.A.)

The rush and excitement of the daily news seems far removed from the long-term commitments of scholarly research in university libraries and laboratories. But, in fact, newspapers and TV can have very powerful effects on the academic research agenda. Daily decisions by news organisations about topics to emphasize, to mention or to ignore influence three important groups:

- Government officials, both those elected representatives and career public officials whose priorities and budget decisions determine the level of funding from public money for various types of research.
- The general public, or at least the active, informed portion of the public, whose support or lack of support, is the essential backdrop in democratic societies for public funding of various kinds of research.
- Researchers themselves who make most of the strategic and tactical decisions about where and how to proceed in any line of scholarly and scientific inquiry.

Even modest media influence among these groups can significantly effect on the research agenda.

Good basic research can have many origins, often far removed from the formal stereotypes of how scientists and scholars work. Good research depends on a strong sense of curiosity and the tenacity to pursue a theoretical line of inquiry.

News topics can be a key sources of ideas for research, especially news about problems that suggests particular applications of expertise. Thoughtful, careful work on these topics can contribute both to basic research and social progress.

Points for Further Reflection

- How can governments be encouraged to continue funding basic research so that universities are major agents of economic growth?
- Can governments in the developing world manage to contribute a reasonable percentage of their GNP to promote scholarship and capacity-building in research?
- What strategies help to break the isolation of researchers in the developing world? e.g. Twining and sandwich post-graduate programmes?
- How can governments, especially those in the developing countries, have access to the benefits of technology and virtual learning?
- How can research institutes *outside* the higher education context co-operate with those *inside* the system to promote the principle of the universality of knowledge?
- How can training for research ensure that expertise is acquired in both the natural and social sciences in order to fully understand the social impact of knowledge?
- What guidelines are needed to ensure the ethical conduct of research?
- How can major NGOs in the Sciences and Social Sciences (e.g. ICSU and ISSC) collaborate more closely to study major global issues (e.g. population, environmental changes)?

20

The Contribution of Higher Education to the Education System as a Whole

Viewpoints: Argentina, China, Qatar, Forum for African Women Educationalists (FAWE), Germany, United States of America, Republic of Namibia

Higher education has a major role in the education system as a whole, particularly in this period of rapid and revolutionary readjustment of such systems everywhere. Social changes, frequently technologically driven, are requiring major education reforms as societies now need education systems capable of playing the key role in this period of global development. The requirements of quality education and training for the whole generation of students, together with the growing implementation of lifelong learning for all, place radically different demands on all education systems and higher education will have to adjust to this.

Higher education needs to contribute both conceptually and in the preparation of personnel. Conceptually through: contribution to the redevelopment of the school curriculum; the analysis and evaluation of education systems; through anticipatory thinking on the evolution of education, and through the development of co-operative networks. A particular priority exists for the education of girls and women. In personnel; through the preparation of teachers; of specialists for the whole field of education, formal and non-formal; in the development of continuing professional education, including its own personnel.

Today, higher education, emphasizing growth of student numbers and finance, requires a more general commitment to the well-being of education as a whole. For this, the contribution of research to improved educational practice is vital, along with the call for a "new academic covenant" which provides for a major reassessment, involving the crucial intellectual role of universities.

This covenant affirms:

- the contribution of higher education to the entire educational system as part of its service function;
- the potential of Open and Distance Learning for access;
- teacher education as a continuous enterprise;
- the role of higher education in reshaping school curriculum;
- the importance of training experts in lifelong learning methods;
- the need to link research on education to practice;
- the need for research on all areas of education;
- the importance of all levels of education for women and girls;
- the role of higher education in evaluating educational systems;
- its role in anticipating the needs of education in the future;
- the benefits of co-operative educational networks;
- the desirability for interaction between education scholars and experts in other disciplines;
- the need for universities to cater for adult learners by: recognizing previous educational achievement, providing outreach services to the community,

assuring interdisciplinary research on all aspects of adult learning, and creating flexible opportunities for these learners.

- ❑ How Higher Education can Contribute to the Development of Education in General: The Latin American Experience Mrs. Cecilia Braslavsky (Argentina)

While the role of education in improving people's quality of life has been revalued throughout Latin America and policies for reform have been drawn up, there are still not sufficient conditions to guarantee the quality of education itself. There is also an urgent need to reinvent education. In other words, there is a conviction that it is no longer a question of trying to revive the schools and education systems invented in the late 19th century and expanded in the 20th century, but of inventing another institutional model able to embrace new teaching practices.

Two questions arise, *First, who can do this? Second, how can this invention be actually translated into action?*

In the past, the state played a fundamental role in both issues. The history of Latin American education results from the creative ability of national states, whose weakness or strength was reflected in their schools and educational systems. But participation by Latin American national states in the 1990s is significantly different from the leading role they played in the foundation and expansion of education systems. Previously, they were leading figures which hindered, reshaped and controlled many non-government initiatives. Not without tensions or ambiguities, they are now trying to be promoters and guarantors of a scenario where more actors converge to find better solutions to problems and to facilitate the required reinvention of education.

So, higher education institutions now act in a different context. Much more than before they need to help reinvent education through reflection and active critical analysis. They should be the leading figures in the renewal of education as a whole, together with national ministries, other organisations and social actors.

But, the new question is whether they really do play this role.

❑ Training Quality School Teachers
Prof. Y.P. Chung (China)

The three intellectual levels of school teachers

At the basic level, schoolteachers must maintain and perpetuate the education system itself. However, schoolteachers are not just custodians. We have observed schoolteachers whose major concerns are to maintain discipline and to "cover" the examination syllabus. They reject disadvantaged or problem students. As a result, the education system will generate a submissive generation with little self-confidence. Students will be good at following orders, but timid and unimaginative.

A passive generation good at exams is not too difficult to produce. However, basic education should nurture creative minds. This is particularly important in the era of information technology and the new workplace. We need a generation that is able to solve problems, to master information technology and to collaborate with peers. The quality of education has become the focus of attention in many places where general basic education has been achieved. However, quality education depends very much on the quality of teachers. We need confident schoolteachers with good subject knowledge and teaching skills.

Quality education should progress even beyond the effective imparting of knowledge and the cultivation of creative minds to instil a genuine concern for human development: social equity, health, environment, and world peace. Schoolteachers should include this perspective in their teaching and also reflect on the existing education system. *But, would this be too difficult for schoolteachers who have never been to the university?*

❑ Teaching in Qatar: A Feminine Profession
Dr. Darwish Ghuloom Al-Emadi (Qatar)

Qatari female employees (mainly teachers, head mistresses) have become far more numerous than males. This is due to two factors:

- more females graduate from the University of Qatar, especially from the Faculty of Education;

- the conservative nature of the country where the segregated school system provides females with a more socially acceptable work environment.

Although male and female pupil numbers are close, the number of female teachers is more than double that of male teachers. This is because grades 1-5 of both sexes are taught by women who are considered more efficient in dealing with kids at this stage. Consequently:

1. The total number of female employees in the school system is very close to the total number of female university graduates. This is due to the fact that, socially and culturally, the working environment at school appeals to female graduates and is acceptable to various social groups.
2. The sharp increase in the number of male employees since 1991 is due to a Law Act by which all male graduates from Art Faculties (Education, Humanities and Sharia) joint the Ministry of Education Prior to this, most male graduates preferred to work in other areas and that explains the low number of Qatari male teachers prior to 1990, compared to the number of male graduates.

❑ Eliminating Gender Disparities in Education: the Role of Higher Education
Dr. Eddah Gachukia—Forum for African Women Educationlists (FAWE)

Higher education institutions in Africa are generally characterized by high quantative expansion and serious financial constraints. They have also been slow in adapting to changing social and economic environments. As a result, there has been little or no diversification of structures or programmes. Many universities still teach and offer the courses of the 1960s, while the traditional mentality that the university is a male domain persists.

African universities, and indeed institutions of higher learning everywhere, cannot escape the major challenges of democratization, globalization, regionalization and marginalization. Faced with these, they require a new vision that combines two aspects. First, the universal acceptance of programmes that are all-inclusive (gender sensitive) and, second, more relevant programmes that prepare students for life. Higher education institutions must continue to set the pace for the social, political and economic development of each country and contribute to the education of citizens.

All countries must continue to redress gender imbalances in education at all levels. As stated in Article 33 of the World Declaration on Education for All, *"The most urgent priority is to ensure access to, and improve the quality of education for girls and women, and to remove every obstacle that hampers their participation."*

Removing the obstacles is a continuous process that requires strong partnerships and, most importantly, the development of a common vision for education.

❑ Universities as Lifelong Learning Institutions
Dr. In a Grieb (Germany)

The *CONFITEA Conference on Adult Education (Hamburg, 1997)* adopted an *Agenda for the Future,* which specified ways to open schools, colleges and universities to adult learners.

Point 9 of the *Mumbai Statement on Lifelong Learning, Active Citizenship and the Reform of Higher Education (University of Mumbai, India, 1998)* states that the transformation of institutions into genuine lifelong learning establishments requires a holistic approach which:

- supports the institution becoming a lifelong learning community itself;
- integrates academic, financial and administrative elements;
- provides structures which are responsible for organizational, staff, student and curriculum development and community engagement;
- aligns the various supportive structures such as academic information systems, library provision and learning technologies to the new mission of universities in learning societies.

To follow up the World Conference on Higher Education, national systems and universities should ensure that this approach is widely adopted.

❑ Non-Formal Basic Education (NFBE): A Priority Area
Dr. Daniel A. Wagner (U.S.A.)

Despite significant public attention over several decades, illiteracy and the non-formal basic education needs of out-of-school youth and adults have received relatively little attention, and even fewer resources (human or fiscal) from universities and research institutes.

Seven principles for action are:

1. Low literate youth and adults are a chronic feature of the global educational landscape;
2. Illiteracy and low literacy are inextricably linked to agricultural and worker productivity, fertility and infant mortality, and other non-educational sectors;
3. Accountability is central to the future of successful literacy and NFBE programmes;
4. Increased professionalization is at the centre of any progress is literacy work;
5. Move away from a "one size fits all" approach to literacy;
6. "Truth in advertising" should be a programmatic goal;
7. Advanced technologies are now too cheap to ignore in the future of adult literacy work.

These principles suggest areas where higher education can play an even greater role in this central domain of educational development—the reduction of global illiteracy.

❑ Education for Transformation: the Global Need for Promethean Change
Mr. B.J. Wentworth (Republic of Namibia)

In areas of human development in which we seek to improve our capacities as "tool maker", higher education recalls the cultural heritage of the Greek figure of Prometheus. We remember this western deity primarily as the Firebearer, who stole fire from heaven for man's use and who taught man the practical arts of mathematics, metallurgy, navigation and medicine. Prometheus becomes the god of light and reason, an appropriate symbol of the role of higher education, at least in western industrial culture. Prometheus, whose name means forethought or anticipation, symbolizes higher education's role of advancing "tool-intelligence", the human trait which has become the exclusive indicator of development in the modern world.

But in many other areas (especially those which pertain directly to values, principles of individual and group behaviour), higher education seems to have performed well as an agent of stability, homogeneity and continuity, but poorly—or not at all—as an agent of change. Prometheus symbolizes the human power to foresee consequences, not just in manipulative or tool—intelligence behaviour, but in areas where humans are supposed to be wise and prudent as well. We are not just *homo faber*—man the tool maker—but homo *sapiens* as well. We are "Man the wise".

The *Framework for Priority Action for Change and Development in Higher Education* states that: 'higher education institutions must regard ethical, as well as scientific rigour, as indispensable in all their activities', ... and should include 'a sharp sense of the social pertinence of studies and of their anticipatory function' and also should include 'fundamentals of human ethics, applied to each profession and to all areas of human endeavour.' These are, themselves, Promethean goals.

Points for Further Reflection

- Since Jomtien, has higher education strengthened its role in relation to the other levels of education?
- What are the major challenges for higher education systems with regard to teacher training (formal and non-formal)?
- Is current research in the educational sciences meeting the key needs of education systems?
- What lessons can be drawn from good practice across various regions (i.e. where there are good linkages

between higher education and other levels of the education system)?

- What partnerships (e.g. government, private sector/ industry, NGOs, UNESCO Chairs) are necessary to ensure these linkages?
- What mechanisms are required at the system level?
- What are the necessary measures to be adopted for the purpose of certification and recognition through non-formal education (NFE) systems?

21

Women and Higher Education

Viewpoints: Pakistan, Swedish International Development Co-operation Agency (SIDA), Nambia, Chile, Inter-American Organization for Higher Education (IOHE), International Federation of University Women (IFUW), Lebanon, India, Uganda, Bulgaria, Brazil, Forum for African Women Educationalists (FAWE).

The debate constituted a stocktaking of the factors related to women's access to and participation in higher education. It also studied the contribution of women graduates to the development dynamic across different regions and socio-economic and cultural contexts.

Over the past decade, and as secondary enrolments increase, many more women have entered post-secondary education. In certain countries (e.g. Australia, Canada) female enrolments exceed those of men. In others (e.g. Botswana, China), the rate of enrolment has doubled on even tripled. These are positive signs, though women still tend to enrol in fields such as education and nursing and they are very under represented in science and technology.

In contrast, much needs to be done in all regions to improve the presence of women in the decision-making process of higher education itself. In posts such as vice-chancellor, rector and head of department, women are far too few.

Many of the recognized social barriers preventing women's advancement have their origins in cultural attitudes which must be reassessed and attenuated to acknowledge the crucial role played by women in social development as citizens and professionals. This implies that social responsibility and power must be more equally shared between the sexes.

The future should focus on the mainstreaming of the gender issue, on the elimination of cultural barriers related to women's progress and on the promotion of shared social and professional decision-making.

❑ Remarks of the Chairperson
Dr. Attiya Inayatullah (Pakistan)

If the Beijing Conference focused world attention on gender, then the World Conference on Higher Education must focus on the future of this field so as to promote continuous change. To participate, women need to be fully aware of their rights in every area—as citizens or as professionals. This will require large-scale capacity building action so that they acquire all necessary skills for their various roles.

Principal strategies for the future should be:

- to promote advocacy regarding women's access to higher education;
- to enhance the presence of women at the decision-making levels of this sector;
- to encourage better employment possibilities for graduate women.

Keynote Presentation

❑ Making Universities Gender Aware: The Swedish Experience
Dr. Berit Olsson (Swedish International Development Co-operation Agency—SIDA)
Prof. Christina Ullenius (University College of Karlstad)

The issue of gender must constitute a primary concern for governments. This is not only a question of justice but also of democracy and academic quality. It cannot be viewed as an issue for developing countries alone since the absence of women in decision-making is a general phenomenon which is evident in all regions of the world. For this reason, everyone can learn from dialogue on this question.

Gender research is important in order to expose the mechanisms based on culture and traditions which form our society. This merits status as a separate field of study which should then be mainstreamed throughout the university curricula.

Social attitudes have started to change but it is, as yet, too early to see the full impact of this. Quotas and such strategies still have their place. The Swedish government has successfully created new academic positions exclusively for women so that a target of 10% female professors is to be reached within the next ten years. Such measures may be controversial but they remain necessary until different thinking on gender becomes evident.

Institutional Viewpoints from Universities, the Professoriate, NGOs and IGOs

❑ Prof. Peter Katjavivi (Namibia)

Namibia has chosen to invest foremost in education meeting the basic requirements of the country. The education given has to be economically profitable, which means that priority is given to courses giving maximum social, cultural and economic return. Women in higher education can thus become a neglected area in terms of the resources invested therein. Nevertheless, it is crucial for the empowerment of women in the field of social decision-making.

The future agenda must be more just—but how will this happen? At the present time, the problems are well known, but the solutions remain uncertain.

❑ Dr. Maria Irigoin (Chile) and the Inter-American Organization for Higher Education (IOHE)

Patience is required to attain greater participation of women in power and decision-making since the world is male-dominated in many of its principal structures of governance. Glass ceilings are common and gender is still not properly recognized as an academic domain in its own right; yet the contribution of women to development cannot be ignored, nor can gender be separated from democracy and social equity. The empowerment of women is essential to attain the goals necessary for social development.

- Mrs. Linda Souter (Canada-International Federation of University Women)

Profound attitudinal change is now urgent. Some 23 years after the first conference on women, higher education remains a very male-dominated—and even old-fashioned—culture. Governments and universities must work together to bring about the attitudinal change which is long overdue. Advocacy and research are two powerful factors leading to this change and are areas where NGOs have gained special expertise.

- Prof. Federico Mayor (Spain—Director-General of UNESCO, 1987-1999)

Higher education is the sector where the presence of women in decision-making is very weak—this is unacceptable in a truly democratic society and attests to the need for attitudinal change.

Power-sharing, in any field, is difficult for men for historical reasons. They must learn to change in this regard as a new paradigm is required for sustainable human development—one which is based on equal responsibility for women and men and so may achieve better results than at present. *Daring to share* would indeed be the key challenge for the coming years.

Regional Viewpoints

- Dr. Joy Kwesiga (Uganda)

In Sub-Saharan Africa, the cultural context has posed great problems for women entering or advancing in higher education: traditional domestic barriers, newer problems such as changing social lifestyles, economic obstacles such as tuition fees and the pressure to work. Women are reluctant to tackle the hard road towards a successful academic career.

Goals must be ambitious, and a variety of strategies are vital; exposure to international experience in the gender debate, research, legislation, and advocacy at the secondary school level. A shift in management and monitoring is needed so that competence is valued over mere hierarchy and so that women's confidence can grow.

❑ Dr. Binod Khadria (India)

In Asia and elsewhere, the higher education sector is marked by profound social divisions as to which classes and races can have access to advanced studies.

The barriers faced by women are numerous and complex. For instance, parenthood is much more constraining for women than for men and women tend to remain in crucial support positions to successful men—in politics, in business, in science.

As the world enters a period of post-access—and even of post-gender—society must guard against facile explanations whereby women's progress is simply a question of time.

❑ Prof. Mouna Mourad (Lebanon)

The Arab States, which are patriarchal societies with strong cultural and religious traditions, have created stereotypes of women as being physiologically and intellectually inferior to men. Arab women face an absence of legislation to cover their interests, of counselling and of financial independence, as well as a lack of infrastructure allowing them to combine their personal and professional lives. In many instance, they are unaware of their rights'.

One key role of higher education is thus to encourage women to be confident in knowing that they have the possibility—and responsibility—to contribute to the sustainable development of their societies. Certain strategies are important to create a critical mass of women ready to direct change: advocacy, research on gender, training in management skills—and, in particular, contact with international developments in these areas.

❑ Prof. Ralitsa Muharska (Bulgaria)

Prior to 1990, women in Eastern and Central Europe were considered as citizens with the same rights and expectations as men. In the academic world, nothing in theory prevented women from rising to posts as professors, as researchers and even, albeit in limited numbers, as rectors. In short, the political climate provided a large degree of equality to women.

The debate on gender and on its many complex aspects just did not take place. This is seen as a Western import and time will be required to construct the infrastructure needed to assure the advocacy, research and training necessary to advance the cause of women in these countries in the coming years. Progress has been incrementally slow and the field of Women's Studies has struggled for survival, being regarded as a marginal and inferior discipline. Countries in transition are still defining their own specific culture of feminism and, to this end, international exchanges are essential.

❑ Prof. Maria D'Avila Neto (Brazil)

The cultural and religious heritage of Latin America has tended to stereotype women in clearly defined roles which were difficult to reject of modernize. Higher education in the developing world must be anchored in the reality of social development—*inter alia,* in human rights, illiteracy, community health, and in changing patterns in family life and in employment. In Brazil, only 11% of the 150 million population accedes to higher education. Such social exclusion is particularly detrimental for women and especially the disadvantaged. Their empowerment depends on education, often at the most basic level. As governments struggle to cope with these problems, higher education institutions must modernize to re-orient their research to address the needs of local communities.

Special Presentations

❑ Association of African Universities (AAU)

In Africa, women constitute a clear minority both in student enrolment (25%) and staff employment (20% approx.). This must now be the main concern of advocacy groups. Since universities play such a profound role in national development throughout Africa in generating the needed human power and competencies, this issue must be a priority.

The main reasons for low participation of women in higher education, are, *inter alia,* social impediments, lack of role models, lack of mentoring, lack of self-confidence, sexual harassment, and gender-insensitive regulations. Quota systems for admission, provision of bursaries for female students, and Science clinics for girls are some of the remedial strategies that have been successful.

❑ Forum for African Women Educationalists (FAWE)

Five points of intervention are crucial to maximize women's representation in higher education: *access, participation, pedagogy, administration and management, and networking.* Continuing strategies must include: affirmative action, a system of loans and scholarships for women and clear codes of conduct against sexual harassment.

When include competent women in administration and management, universities provide important role models for their students and recognize women's presence and qualifications. Processes of recruitment and promotion have to be transparent and indisputable. Having women at all levels of higher education facilitates network-building.

Points for Further Reflection

- Is gender now a tenet of higher education policy at both systemic and institutional levels?
- What are the cultural barriers to women's presence in higher education and how can these be eliminated?
- What strategies can best help effect attitudinal change with regard to women's empowerment through higher education?
- **How to promote strategies for advocacy?**

(e.g. national, regional and international observatories to monitor the advancement of women in higher education; reviewing the effectiveness of existing legal instruments; stimulating NGO support for a *Charter of Commitment to Gender Equity in Higher Education*)

- ❑ How to increase women's presence in decision-making?

(e.g. establishing senior staff committees and setting up Equal Employment Opportunities offices (EEO) in institutions to monitor appointments; ensuring that career guidance services focus on women; highlighting the value of women as role models and pathfinders).

- ❑ How to ensure that, by 2010, women represent 50% of:
  - higher education enrolments
  - executive managerial and academic posts
  - the members of higher education governing bodies (senates, councils, etc.)?

22

Promoting a Culture of Peace

Viewpoints: United States of America, Costa Rica, Saudi Arabia, Ghana, Croatia

The need to construct a new paradigm for peace in the post-Cold War era and the involvement of universities around the world in this process will be the major educational imperatives in the future.

Violence has taken on a new face globally with the end of the Cold War. No longer is confrontation between superpowers the central issue of war and peace. Today, intrasocietal violence-violence within nations-overshadows violence that pits nation against nation.

However, intrasocietal violence is not always confined within national borders. As the experiences in Rwanda, Burundi, the Republic of Congo, Sri Lanka, and the Balkans demonstrate, intrasocietal violence can easily spill across communities and boundaries miring regions in intersocietal conflict.

In the world today, there are 3500 population groups that describe themselves as "nations" while only 185 such groups are actively recognized as "nation states" by the international community. The potential for intersocietal and intrasocietal conflict involving a large number of these 3500 population groups is enormous and provides a powerful rationale for the vigorous promotion of a Culture of Peace.

Other factors which are very important in the promotion of a Culture of Peace include environmental concerns, sustainable economic development, solutions for the increasing number of refugees and the promotion of international relations among and between countries.

Development of a new paradigm for peace in response to the challenges of increased societal violence is vital. Development of a worldwide Culture of Peace is required. The participation of universities in creating and maintaining the new paradigm, in fostering a Culture of Peace, can be a critical component.

The tools of the past used by nations to solve conflict—war and diplomacy—are no longer appropriate, nor sufficient in their new global environment. Military power have severe limits when it comes to arresting violence. When the roots of conflict extend beyond states jockeying for power over territory—often the end result of deep-set enmities—diplomacy too can have limits.

Thus, the challenge today in dealing with violence is the establishment of a Culture of Peace in nations and providing education that causes nations and their people to learn ways to live in peace with each other.

Using education as a tool for transformation of the world from violence to peace has been a traditional mission of UNESCO as well as of IAUP. It is now important to enrich this mission by having universities become more fully engaged in the process. The goal is to make it imperative for educators around the world to assist in building societal resistance to violence through peace education.

Regional Viewpoint

❑ Universities as Agents of a Culture of Peace
Dr. Oscar Arias (Costa Rica)

Universities have a political role in the challenge to establish a Culture of Peace. In Latin America, we shall never forget the contribution of students to the struggle against dictatorships; in the United States, the academy fought hard for civil rights; in Africa and Asia, the political independence of many countries owes much to the forward-thinking commitment of academics.

Particular note should be paid to the efforts of universities to bring about disarmament and demilitarization, which are core aspects of a Culture of Peace. These efforts are never properly resourced yet they can reach their objectives, for example:

- in Panama, a campaign to alter the Constitution so as to abandon a standing army finally succeeded—as did a similar move in Costa Rica in 1949;
- a current campaign, rather promising, is urging Haiti to do the same;
- the promotion of an International Caode of Conduct against the Transfer of Weapons has been launched in collaboration with various experts and institutions, all Nobel Peace Prize winners;
- active opposition to the transfer of hi-tech weapons from the United States and other industrialized countries to Latin America which could unleash an expensive arms race in the region;
- the convening of an international conference on disarmament and demilitarization in Sub-Saharan Africa.

The original motto of the University of San Carlos de Guatemala, the oldest in Central America reads: *Id and Education for All.* Perhaps this conference should adopt a similar motto for all the universities of the world: *Id, Education, Freedom and Peace for All.* In this way, we could take the first step towards transforming higher education into the conscience of humanity.

❑ Tolerance and Arab-Islamic Societies Today
Prof. Saleh Al-Mani (Saudi Arabia)

While the Arab-Islamic state of yesterday was weak and centred in major cities and towns, the new state in our region exercises tremendous impact on the life of its citizens, majority and minority alike. Tensions in nation building have tempted some supporters of the regimes to call for the suppression of certain minority rights. While some leaders were tempted to do this, international and Western influence (sometimes hegemonic) persuaded them against such action. In other instances, external powers have looked the other way, particularly if their own allies committed violations.

While some leaders may have adopted inclusive policies, they were far from following the liberal views of Voltaire and John Locke on religious and cultural tolerance. Westernization of the Arab and Islamic state system has led in theory to equal economic membership in society, rather than equal political participation. Since there was no civil political rights for the majority (religious and ethnic), there were likewise no political rights for minorities.

While collective intolerance may have been kept at bay, individual intolerance in Arab societies began to be apparent. Two factors caused this.

Firstly, the change process brought different workers (particularly government white-collar workers) to compete with one another for the same jobs. The level of education of applicants, naturally, influenced employee selection. Those from regions long in touch with the outside world benefited from more developed modern educational facilities and fared better than the others who did not have access to modern schooling.

Secondly, with the huge influx of people from the countryside to the cities, the new immigrants could not afford better housing or good education, at least for the first generation. Urbanization began to create social cleavages between old immigrants and the new ones. This phenomenon exists in many Arab countries, as well as elsewhere in the third world. This process may lead to future personal forms of intolerance, or a differentiation between the "in-groups and out-groups".

❑ The Culture of Peace in Sub-Saharan Africa
Prof. George Benneh (Ghana)

In Africa, there is the tendency to explain armed conflicts simply in terms of ethnic rivalries. But, at the heart of these conflicts is the question of how the state manages its business in the new global society which is moving towards a multi-cultural, pluralistic system. Underlying these conflicts are issues of good governance, devolution of power (from a highly centralized and personalized system of government to a decentralized one which ensures the right to effective participation in the economic and political life of a country), an equitable share of the fruits of development among the ethnic groups in a multi-ethnic state, and reducing inequality and ethnic social disparities. In this respect, the prevention of armed conflicts ultimately requires radical socio-economic and political reforms.

The impact of various forms of conflict on African development in this first decade after the Cold War has certainly not been positive. Political stability and infrastructure for development (such as buildings, roads and highly-trained human lives) have been the most obvious victims. The conflicts have also unleashed an enormous flood of displaced people and refugees whose immediate survival needs defy the combined resources of humanitarian agencies all over the world. Often, the refugee menace spills over into neighbouring states causing fresh violence and widening its scope. Africa accounts for 13 million out of the world's 20 million displaced persons.

The future development of sub-Saharan Africa depends on peace and stability in the region. The costs of armed conflicts are high in terms of human suffering and poverty, which they engender. Conflicts are part of human existence. It is, however, important that conflicts are transformed from those that lead to violence into those that find expression in persuasion and arguments. The best place to promote this culture is the University.

❑ Preparing Teachers for a Culture of Peace
Dr. Betty A. Reardon (U.S.A.)

UNESCO, in its mission to construct "the foundations of peace", could undertake some or all of the following:

- Set up a task force to design and develop a core curriculum for teacher education;
- Establish, in co-operation with IAUP and the UNESCO Associated Universities, a global network of teacher education institutions to specify and develop the proposals of the task force in culturally appropriate ways, placing special emphasis on *training*.
- Co-ordinate a survey, conducted by ministries of education, to identify available curricula and practices in Teacher Education for a Culture of Peace, especially in the areas of conflict resolution, peace studies, human rights education and gender equality.

Ministries of education, to better prepare the citizenry of their respective countries for a culture of peace, could:

- Hold national conferences on teacher education to review and discuss the findings of the surveys on curricula and practices for a Culture of Peace, identify needs and design programmes for relevant preservice and in-service teacher education.
- Establish a national panel of experts to work with individual universities and other teacher education institutions to facilitate implementation of the UNESCO task force proposals and the practices devised by the teacher education network of the UNESCO Associated Universities.

Educational and professional associations, in co-operation with IAUP and other international education NGOs, could:

- Set up professional commissions on Teacher Education for a Culture of Peace to formulate suggestions for ministries of education and to provide curriculum change and development services for teacher education institutions.
- Sponsor and organize periodic intensive in-service courses in Education for a Culture of Peace at national and regional levels.

❑ Information Technologies and the Culture of Peace: A view from the Balkans
Prof. Enver Sehovic (Croatia)

My region has suffered severely from war. A development programme to assist Croatia and Bosnia and Herzegovina in overcoming their problems and to open a new page in their relations, is in preparation. Its main points are:

- Political stability could be attained if priority is given to development. The Information Society programme, adapted to local conditions and requirements, is proposed as a platform for further actions.
- Being more developed, and having already deployed an advanced communication infrastructure, Croatia should help Bosnia and Herzegovina so that it also proceeds along the same path. Assistance should he given to Bosnia and Herzegovina to design and develop its own high-speed network, and to become connected to similar networks worldwide. By extending the broadband pilot network toward Bosnia and Herzegovina, and the involving the Croatian Academic and Research Network (CARNet) in the project, a reasonably wide and interconnected infrastructure will be created in the two countries. Fair co-operation, in which the interests of both parties will be respected, and where neither side will be patronized, is essential.
- Modernizing economies and administrations, IT-based support to research, education, health care, culture, and civil society programmes, all offer tremendous possibilities for co-operation. Concrete international support for these activities is anticipated.
- The Inter-University Centre in Dubrovnik, gathering some 200 universities worldwide, is supposed to play a major role in these programmes. It can provide a framework for very wide international academic co-operation.

This Thematic Debate is the result of activities undertaken in the IAUP/UN Commission on Disarmament

Education, Conflict Resolution and Peace. Every possible effort should be made to ensure that participating scholars remain together. Multidisciplinary programmes with an IT element for their joint endeavours should be furthered.

Points for Further Reflection

- What are the main elements of a new *paradigm of peace* in today's society?
- A *Culture of Peace* should bring together opinion-builders, policy-makers and educators. How can this be done effectively within the social and educational processes?
- How can *Peace Education* (e.g. human rights, inter-cultural relations) be mainstreamed across the higher education curriculum?
- Taking into account the character and needs of specific socio-cultural contexts, how can university research, training and service contribute to fostering a Culture of Peace in the local community?
- What is the role of international academic co-operation in fostering a Culture of Peace?
- In particular, how can advances in information and communication technologies, including INTERNET, be used in higher education to promote a Culture of Peace?

23

Mobilizing the Power of Culture

Viewpoints: Council on International Educational Exchange (CIEE), Benin, European Association for International Education (EAIE), Spain, United States of America, France

The 1990s have been marked by very considerable and rapid change as national cultures have been drawn into new global inter-connections. There are new challenges, new risks, new uncertainties and new struggles. The issue though is not just one of adopting new policies, but one of re-conceiving policies so that they are effective in an environment of inter-dependence and are effective at a time in which the imperatives of promoting better mutual appreciation between cultures, of elimination stereotypes and of forging peace between people is of supreme importance.

In this scenario, universities too need to play a different role, because young people must be able to build meaningful connections with their inherited cultures as they increasingly find it hard to adapt to the values which drove the cultures of yesterday. So it is time to re-examine our educational systems and formulate new ways of addressing the needs and aspirations of young people in a rapidly changing world. It is essential to examine how universities can fulfil this role. Their curricula and methodology are key tools by which they can achieve their objectives. Their role should be to articulate cultural policies in a world where cultural diversity has emerged as a crucial social factor and they should be capable of developing co-operative strategies which involve higher education and ensure that cultural heritage and values are preserved. They must be able to broaden the context in which education is imparted, without focusing primarily on technique. Universities must revamp their educational agendas so as to be able to inform young people about "other culture—those of the past as well as those different from our own.

How universities fulfil this role becomes a paramount question. Recalling the impact of *Our Creative Diversity* (the Report of the World Commission on Culture and Development) and the education/culture linkage emphasized by the *Intergovernmental Conference on Cultural Policies for Development* (Stockholm, 1998), a number of key questions for discussion are:

- How well do educational systems inform young people about other cultures?
- Can Arts education be broadened to include understanding of the contexts in which art forms originated and flourished?
- Can intercultural education have a central role in today's global world dominated by cyberspace?
- How can universities tackle these issues via research and academic activity?
- Can universities work more closely with cultural heritage experts?

Today, the need to deal constructively with cultural diversity is rapidly becoming a central issue in education. Sociocultural heterogeneity is growing due to:

- change in the organization of the world economy which has impacted on migration trends;
- expanded transport and communication systems which have facilitated mobility and information exchange;

- worldwide attention to human rights which has generated many culture-specific interest groups.

As the Third Millennium dawns, countries need to foster cultural pluralism amongst their peoples. Furthermore, a global "civil consensus" would help to recognize the validity of both the common and distinctive aspects of our lives.

Scientific anthropological knowledge should be the base for multicultural education programmes to ensure that pedagogical approaches are not culture-specific. Anthropology through its interdisciplinary potential, enables us to understand the differences and similarities of humankind. This is the very essence of multiculturalism—thus, the mission of multicultural education should be to better understand the dynamics of this phenomenon to promote social harmony. Anthropology is about to have its day.

❑ Education and Culture
Prof. Nabil El-Haggar (France)

What is the university's role in the relationship between education and culture? The university must affirm that culture is not merely entertainment but an elevation of the spirit, achieved as much by objective, rational knowledge as by a subjective, artistic and multifaceted approach to the world.

Culture is no longer a fundamental concern of society. Its resources are generally low and given to activities which are socially and politically profitable. Yet, thanks to academics, artists and intellectuals, genuine cultural development is occurring. These are the "gatekeepers" of culture and the university remains the place were ideas are confronted and views are exchanged.

Today, the university has three responsibilities:

- it preserves knowledge and learning via a critical approach which is a precondition for the ability to see a subject in perspective and with a deep understanding that lasts throughout life;
- it can promote culture among citizens other than students; as a public institution, it should be open

to all in a spirit of freedom and impartiality which welcomes debate on controversial issues;

- as an institution, it can reiterate that education and culture make possible the full exercise of citizenship and the realization of one's fill potential.

But one question still baffles us: *How can we ensure that science, research, artistic activity, scholarship and technical skills (all products of the intelligence and imagination) better serve human progress?*

Points for Further Reflection

- How can higher education institutions exploit their own specific cultural identity?
- Can-and should-essential cultural issues (e.g. culture and identity, culture and human rights, cultural heritage, etc.) be incorporated into a basic university education?
- Could students undertake voluntary work and internships (to be recognized as credits) with a cultural component as part of understanding their community?
- How can institutions become better "brokers" of cultural communication and exchange?
- Can institutions participate in local cultural industries?
- Can they demonstrate the cross—fertilization between culture and economic activity?
- Can universities network with museums and archives to document the history and patrimony of their context?
- How can institutions best fulfil their cultural mandate i.e. to give students and awareness of "the other" and of "the self"?
- How can the cultural responsibilities of universities be promoted via research?
- How can universities construct a new cultural paradigm for the 21st Century?

- Research on the Cultural Mandate of Universities
  Dr Hilary Callan (European Association for International Education)

  Universities have a dual character:

  - they are cultural products located in a particular physical space; so they partake of that cultural environment and influence it to some degree;
  - as cultural agents, they promote conservation of cultural traditions and they also encourage debate, critical analysis and the juxtaposition of alternative viewpoints-so, they challenge what is taken for granted in a certain cultural context.

For these reasons, they are one of a rare class of institutions (like the performing arts) which make it possible for a culture to critically reflect on itself. Universities located across large-scale cultural or ethnic boundaries and those with strong international outlooks are powerful forces for cultural accommodation, innovation and transformation.

Universities graduate culturally informed and enriched people whose knowledge of "the other" enhances the knowledge of "self".

The capacity (often acquired through academic mobility) to encounter and transact with other cultural realities unleashes a creative imagination which equips people well for our global multicultural world.

But, this role as agents of cultural discovery, education and transformation receives scant attention. A major research programme on the university as "cultural actor" would prove how culture is a critical factor in academic practice. This would have two results:

- better awareness of the cultural importance of universities;
- the creation of paradigms to analyse cultural process inside these institutions.

Can UNESCO and its partners launch this research?

❑ The Cultural Responsibilities of Universities
Prof. Eduard Delgado (Spain)

Cultural policy and the cultural role of higher education have changed everywhere. On the positive side, the Arts are now seen as part of our social fabric and not as social therapy; technology is a creative tool, not merely a means of information storage. However, the non-commercial Arts are neglected and cultural disciplines are rejected for pragmatic career choices.

Universities, with their cultural heritage must be a centre and catalyst for creative activity. Areas where universities can lead are: *conserving patrimony, analysing cultural tourism, promoting the contemporary arts, training for the cultural professions and monitoring arts policies.*

As technology gain ground via open and distance learning it is essential for universities to strengthen their natural "cultural profile". This will:

- *reinforce the significance of their social role;*
- *permit them to manage the new linkages amongst culture, science and technology.*

❑ Anthropology and Multicultural Education
Prof. E. L. Cerroni—Long (U.S.A.)

Assessment of current developments in multicultural education reveals that the specific historical and cultural context in which a programme is implemented affect its character and impact.

Multicultural education can take three forms:

- *it emphasizes the right to recognition and social representation of all marginalized groups;*
- *it celebrates group-specific uniqueness;*
- *it focuses on the common characteristics of our species as the context where diversity can best be documented and understood.*

Regional Viewpoints

❑ Cross Cultural Communication Issues
Dr Gisela Baumgratz-Gangl (Council on International Educational Exchange)

Teaching foreign languages is a matter of transcultural and intercultural communication. Because it is crucial for the issue of professional mobility and for its qualitative assessment, certain inherent dimensions must be understood, notably the culture of teachers and learners and that of the host and guest institutions involved. Immediate examples are exchanges in Europe between different linguistic and cultural settings. For instance, those who study in the French Grande Ecole system gain insight into this country's management culture. On the global scale, the same principles apply.

Thus, it is essential to map the relevant cultural dimensions of a given communication situation where people from different national and cultural origins are put together. If this is done successfully, mobility programmes will enable people to live and work in varying multicultural contexts.

Four aspects require close scrutiny:

- *the context in which a qualification is gained*
- *how this is acquired*
- *its quality*
- *its application inside and outside its own context.*

For each learning situation, transcultural orientation is necessary, so:

- the student must understand the particular location, architecture, infrastructure and internal organization of his/her learning contest;
- the teacher must be aware of his/her own context and that of his/her students.

The ultimate aim is to professionalize mobility programmes. For this to occur, more needs to be known about the internationalization of academic studies—e.g. the status of a particular discipline in a given country and how this is taught. This becomes more complex when a specific field is studied via a foreign language.

Technology offers many new opportunities to professionalize programmes through the availability of multi-media materials and the use of authentic information which explain the learning context. Further research on this will help assess the quality of academic mobility schemes.

❑ African Cultures for Sustainable Development—H.E. Mr Tidjani-Serpos (Benin)

Higher education implies that new knowledge and skills are built upon the continual questioning of the old, as well as on reconsideration of the expertise and heritage accumulated in time and space by earlier generations.

Culture can be mobilized to serve education as a whole including higher education and sustainable development. This process must consider both the wealth of interculturality and the importance of endogenous matters. We must address current questions, ask what solutions were found by previous generations and make a leap forward. Then we can learn how to live peacefully together and how to recognize that your difference adds to my wealth.

In the case of African countries with ancient oral traditions, mobilization of this kind is difficult. Their entry into a world of written culture has led to a deprecation of oral knowledge. Accumulated heritage is diminished, the institutionalization of memory is disorganized and a sense of exclusion can ensue.

Africans with experience of higher education must enrich education at all levels and for all people by making better use of African culture and its values. African universities must develop their structures, curriculum and links with society—but without disowning this patrimony. The principles of the Declaration and Action Plan on Higher Education in Africa must take due note of the region's cultural context.

24

Autonomy, Social Responsibility and Academic Freedom

Viewpoints: South Africa, The Philippines, Chile, Canada, Thailand, Finland

Contemporary universities, like their communities, are in the midst of massive change directed by two central trends: acceleration in the pace of change itself and globalization of the economy and of technology.

Accelerated change is not merely a determinant of both individual and social progress. It also makes the production and dissemination of knowledge a key function in shaping the place of nations in the international order, just as it largely determines the place and status of the individual in society. These developments, as seen by university, mean increasingly heavy responsibility both to provide training and research, investigation and advice as well as such services as consultancies, technology transfer and continuing education.

For 25 years, the forces of modernization have drawn heavily upon higher education. They have also contributed to profound and often radical transformations in that community itself. The drive to mass higher education in the advanced economies and the very substantial growth of institutions and of students in the less advanced economies of the world, confirm this process. This dynamic is likely to continue over the coming decade and beyond. The emergence of "the Learning Society" amongst advanced technology economies (i.d. the establishment of lifelong learning with its concomitant of knowledge updating and renewal for individuals) creates new expectations and demands amongst those who will need—and use—such services and provision.

Growth in demand for higher education since 1975 and its probable continuation have to be viewed against a number of limitations, notably that of public financing. Resource constraint limits the ability of higher education to meet expectations with the quality necessary. Thus, in many countries, the credibility and standing of universities are increasingly subject to question.

One of the most pressing challenges facing universities today is that of resources-how to increase them, to diversify their provenance, to improve both their internal allocation and management and, finally, how to meet the responsibilities society places upon universities whilst maintaining the recognized tradition of autonomy and disinterested service.

Nevertheless, accelerated change presents enormous potential for development as well as formidable challenges. Universities must invest in adaptation, innovation, in developing sensitive and sophisticated systems and methods of management, and in the definition and execution of various alternatives. However, individual universities are far from equal in the resources they command, in the ability of the student body they can attract or in the esteem of their communities. And, whilst society demands that change be rapid, individual universities do not possess the same capacity to respond. Though the strong and those at the 'cutting edge' may remain so, the weak may well be undermined yet further.

The challenges for academic freedom and university autonomy relate to four key issues:

- University Autonomy and Accountability
- University Autonomy and Stakeholders
- Academic Freedom, Ethical Implications and Civic Responsibilities
- Academic Freedom and Entrepreneurial Activities.

Regional Viewpoints

❑ Universities as Partners in Social Decision-Making
Prof. Brenda Gourley (South Africa)

Universities must argue their case in the complex world of today—often with difficulty. Universities may have done their least impressive work on the very subjects where society's needs for greater knowledge and better education are most acute—poverty, violence, war, unemployment. And if universities, wherever they are, with whatever their resources (human and physical) do not seek solutions to pressing human issues, then this could be regarded both as an ethical and intellectual failure. Such solutions will not be found by universities working independently. The world has changed too much for that due to globalization (which looks like a new form of colonisation to poor countries). Businesses have become so big that in many cases their wealth is larger than that of entire countries. They are beginning to realize that the health of the planet, the quality of life of its people and the infrastructure on which they rely for business, are so complex and intertwined that their vulnerability and risks have increased exponentially. Businesses are now partners in seeking solutions.

Nation states also see their autonomy relentessly eroded by globalized economic decision-making, the tides of refugees that make borders irrelevant and the environmental catastrophes that also pay no respect to nationality. They realize that the national level is too small for the big problems and too big for the small problems. They also need partners—so, NGOs, community organizations and such need to work together in this endeavour for a better world.

Institutional leadership must understand and strategize around the realities of our changed environment and orient their institutions accordingly. This demands integrity and the due consideration for the ethical imperatives of social justice. Universities in the conduct of their own internal affairs have not been good examples of social justice in practice. Their staffing and governing structures alone demonstrate that. Let us hope the future will be different.

❑ A Student View on Autonomy and Academic Freedom
Mr. Dennis Longid (The Philippines)

In the Philippines, where we struggle to advance students' democratic rights and welfare, school administrators respond by saying we, the students, are transients. Hence, we have no business in decision and policy-making bodies of universities. We, in the League of Filipino Students (LFS) and the Asian Students Association (ASA) firmly say: "*Students may be transients, but students' rights are not*".

I believe academic freedom is threatened:

- *One*, in terms of access to education. Autonomy means higher fees and costs for students or their being deprived of education;
- *Two*, in terms of the content of education itself. As multinational corporations enter universities, students are limited in what they want to pursue and forced to study matters of vital interest to these companies. There is also the issue of intellectual property;
- *Three*, in opposing this type of autonomy, students are threatened with harassment and repression. Student leaders are denied seats in student unions, policy-making bodies, etc. Some are even barred from enrolling again in their schools. Others go to jail. Legitimate student organizations are being banned; campus publications are closed down. This is another violation of academic freedom.

The LFS and the ASA reiterate their call that education should be free at all levels, and call on all governments to prioritize social services like education, health and housing over debt-servicing and military spending.

❑ Academic Freedom and the Right to Higher Education
Mrs Ximena Erazo (Chile)

The truly democratic society depends on the correct balance between the state, the economy and civil society. One dominant element produces a society driven by a specific philosophy or ideology.

In many developing countries, and in Latin America, the market is too predominant. The state and civil society are better guarantors of democracy, equal opportunity and social justice. The state should be proactive in protecting academic freedom, which can be severely limited in subtle and non-violent ways, and in safeguarding the right to higher education.

This latter element links to other important rights: to education itself, to development, to civil rights and social participation. For this reason, the reform of higher education is a particularly complex issue.

Present reforms in this sector are contradictory. Instead of modernizing institutions and promoting equal access, they constrain universities by severe funding restrictions which inevitably require budget cuts (although higher education is a public service), the elimination of disciplines not considered cost-effective, and the exclusion of citizens unable to pay fees.

Academic freedom respects the right to higher education.

❑ University Autonomy—A Distinct Social Space
Mrs. Lise Bissonnette (Canada)

Today the university should link to socio-economic development. This is easier for North American institutions with their origins in social service. But is the university free to promote its own values and to enjoy its traditional academic freedom?

Not all current changes are due to neo-liberalism alone. After all, the main objective of "1968" was to render the university more socially relevant. Rather, as the economic sector accepts a bigger share of the cost of training and research, the university gains a unique opportunity to reclaim its "*social space*" and attendant responsibilities.

The traditional university can flourish if scholars are protected by academic freedom, if the institution is clearly perceived to be rendering social service and if basic research on development problems continues. Certainly new dangers exist: decision-making driven by budgetary constraints or by the dictates of the labour market, or the failure of rectors to contribute forcefully to public debate.

The solution is for the university to restate its "*social space*"

- *its role in civic debate*
- *its commitment to community development*
- *its respect for culture and intellectual energy.*

There is a great desire, primarily amongst young people, to frequent places and institutions which reaffirm these principles. The main duty of the university has always been to inspire society—rediscovering this historical role and adapting it to the new era is its modern social responsibility.

❑ Definitions of Academic Freedom
Prof. Dr Wichit Srisa—An (Thailand)

Academic freedom remains the central value and condition which both justifies and ensures innovation and organized creativity. This is the central, pervasive, and guiding principle of academic work. It allows the academic community—teaching personnel, students and scholars—to follow its own enquiries independently of political, philosophical or epistemological opinions or beliefs.

Academic freedom is an application of the right to the free holding and expression of opinions with specific reference to researchers, professors, lecturers or students. These rights ar expressly included in all Human Rights treaties. And tl characterize democratic constitutions.

Many countries entrench 'academic freedom' in their constitutions, for example, Austria, Belarus, Bulgaria, Estonia, Finland, Germany, Lithuania, Romania, Slovenia, Spain Sweden, Turkey, and quite recently Thailand (1997).

Thus, academic freedom guarantees the liberty to teach, research, and to express opinions in one's areas of expertise—

and, to do so without fear. An alternative interpretation, more in deeping with the Germanic legal tradition, regards academic freedom as the exemption in the area of academic endeavour and scholarship from government instructions and intervention.

Whatever its particular legal, setting, acaaemic freedom remains the fundamental philosophical premise for the transmission of established knowledge and the generation of new knowledge. It is the optimal condition for the advancement of learning, for underpinning the pursuit of excellence and for applying human creativity to matters of concern to communities (scholarly, economic, industrial and social), which have a stake in higher learning.

❑ Enhancing Autonomy: the Finnish Experience
Mr Olli-Pekka Heinonen (Finland)

Finland is an affluent society which appreciates education and university instruction. This is why we have invested heavily in university education and research in recent years, and will continue to do so.

We have moved from a rather centrally steered university system into a "management by objectives and results" steering system during the last ten years. This has increased the institutional autonomy of our universities which have always had extensive latitude in matters of education and research. The present steering system, together with our new Universities Act, further enhances their autonomy by delegating decision-making power to their own internal administrative and academic structures.

Universities can decide on the choice and structure of faculties. The relaxed steering system does not mean that the government has given away all policy instruments. It can, together with the university and scientific community, set nationally and regionally relevant policy objectives and even target numbers for the graduate output of each university. Setting objectives is not the whole story, however. A credible steering system monitors and evaluates the performance of the universities, and acts on the results.

Accountability is essential. Every other public service demands this. Taxpayers must know what has been done with their money. Of course, there is an evident need to discuss the distance of the steering system; and policy-makers must respect the university's internal activities.

A well-defined strategy safeguards autonomy and academic freedom without compromising social responsibility. Such a strategy should:

- make better use of the university's knowledge production and expertise beyond the world of academia;
- increase the effectiveness and efficiency of all university activities;
- enhance innovation and institution—specific profiles;
- reconcile internal and external and external interests and processes, and, lastly, ensure effective financial management and the profitability of all actions.

Points for Further Reflection

- What are the consequences of an increasingly conditional autonomy for university management and for the role of institutional leadership?
- To what extent is university autonomy compatible with the demand for greater accountability to the public, to students and other stakeholders?
- What is and ought to be the university's role in community development?
- What strategies may be used to involve representatives of civil society in helping the university achieve its mission of service to the community?
- What are the ethical responsibilities subsumed under academic freedom?
- How may the community of higher learning—staff and students alike—develop greater sensitivity to these responsibilities?

- How may the freedom to research and publish be upheld at the same time meet the conditions of confidentiality which an entrepreneurial relationship often demands?
- What safeguards should the university seek from its contractual partners to uphold the terms of its overall mission, its commitment to academic freedom and the concerns of the individual scholar?